O9-BTM-073

CRETE

A full travel guide with 170 colour photographs which will
introduce you to the island 's history, art and folklore.
It guides you round archaeological sites, museums and
others sights, and takes you over 21 routes on the island,
telling you how to get about and where to stay.

Editing and DTP : BARRAGE LTD
Texts: Despina Karakatsni
English Translations: Cox and Solman
Art editing: Fotini Svarna
Photographs: Haitalis Publishing Co. archive

CONTENTS

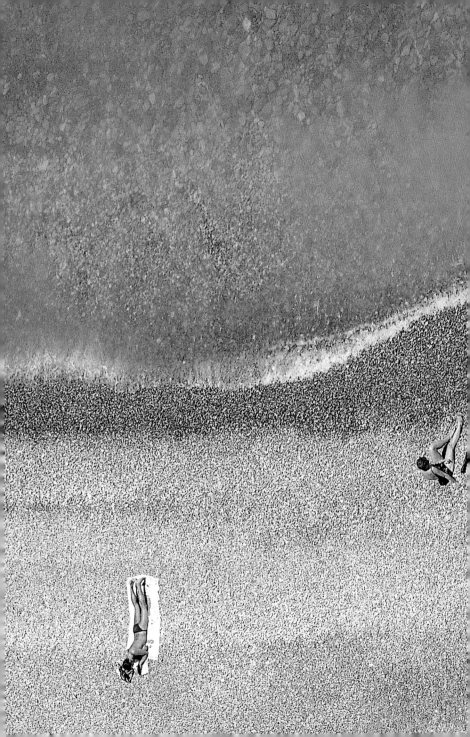

FOREWORD

p. 7 ►
'The Prince with the Lilies' (c.1500 BC). Relief wall-painting found in the Knossos palace. (Irakleio Archaeological Museum)

p. 6
Red-figure krater (mixing vessel) in the Museo Archeologico de Spina in Ferrara (c.470 BC), showing the slaughter of the Minotaur by Theseus.

Crete is the uttermost point of Greece and all Europe; equidistant as it is from Asia, Africa and Europe, it developed into a kind of bridge at the crossroads where three continents meet. It rises from the midst of the ocean in isolation from mainland Greece and the other islands, thus constituting a geographical, historical and cultural entity of its own - one with considerable originality, especially where the folk culture is concerned. Indeed, Crete has sometimes been described as a separate continent.

This island where Zeus was born was the cradle of a great civilisation; it has a truly amazing past - both distant and more recent - which is still reflected in the everyday life of the island people. As the birthplace of Nikos Kazantzakis, Vincenzo Cornaros, El Greco and Eleftherios Venizelos, Crete will enchant the visitor with the wealth of its historical heritage and the authenticity of its folk culture. The vicissitudes of more than 5,000 years of tumultuous history have left their marks on the inhabitants of Crete, who have a unique

character of their own: one which is authentic and unforced, and which is marked by a passion for life and liberty.

In Crete, the visitor will find much to admire, not least the superb works of Minoan art and the architecture of the palaces. Little by little, his travels will lead him through a

labyrinth of prehistory, history and myth - following the thread of the wonderful history of Crete. Furthermore, he will be able to discover for himself the natural beauties of the island and, perhaps more than anything else, the wonders of the Cretan soul as it manifests itself in the many forms of folk culture.

p. 8-9

Past and present live together in harmony in Crete: features of its folk tradition blend into contemporary life.

The history of the island

p. 10

Exhibit from the Numismatic Museum.

The beginnings of the history of Crete fade into the mist where reality and myth meet. The god Zeus, who was born in one of the caves of Crete, looked out from his sanctuary on Mt Ida one day and spied from afar the young princess Europa, on the coast of distant Asia. Taking the form of a white bull, he seduced the maiden, and three sons - Minos, Radamanthys and Sarpedon - were born of their union. Minos, the strongest of the three, founded a powerful sea-borne empire (thalassocracy) and contributed to the growth of the Minoan civilisation, one of the world's greatest. The myths of Daedalus, the Labyrinth, the Minotaur and Theseus were woven around his name.

The Neolithic Period (6000-2600 BC)

p. 11 ▶

Rhyton (drinking-cup) of steatite in the form of a bull's head (1550-1500 BC), found in the little palace at Knossos. The original horns, which have not survived, were of gilded wood, the eyes of rock crystal, and the snout of marble. (Irakleio Archaeological Museum)

The scholars of earlier times argued that the first human settlers arrived in Crete during the Neolithic period. However, traces of human activity which have been identified and evaluated in recent years provide evidence of inhabitation as far back as the Mesolithic or Late Palaeolithic period. The population - widely-scattered during the Neolithic era - lived in the many caves to be found all over Crete (which later retained the nature of holy places) or in primitive houses of brick on stone foundations. The principal occupations of Neolithic man were farming and stock-breeding, with some fishing along the coast. Proof of the fact that these early Cretans were seafarers and traders can be found in the importing of obsidian

from Melos or Nisyros. We know very little about their social organisation: it can be concluded that the social structure was founded on the family, in the broader sense, and that if the community had any leaders they would have been the elders or the priests. There seems to have been little occupational differentiation between men and women with the exception of that imposed by the natural division of labour. As for religion, we can go no further than hypothesis. Perhaps the figurines showing human forms which have been found on Crete (especially at Knossos) may represent the female fertility deity who was worshipped in the East and the Aegean. The most important Neolithic settlement in Crete - and one of the largest in the Eastern Mediterranean - is that which has come to light beneath and around the Minoan palace at Knossos.

The Minoan Period (2600-1100 BC)

p. 12
Neolithic clay figurine, height 14.5 cm., found at Epano Chorio, Ierapetra. (Irakleio Archaeological Museum)

The Neolithic period was followed by the Bronze Age or Minoan era - the name given to it, after the mythical King Minos, by the British archaeologist Sir Arthur Evans, who conducted the excavations at Knossos. The Minoan civilisation, which lasted more than 1,500 years, reached hitherto undreamed of forms of creation and living standards. Evans divided the Minoan era into three periods: a) Early Minoan (2600-2000

BC), b) Middle Minoan (2000-1580 BC) and c) Late Minoan (1580-1100 BC). The period of greatest
prosperity was that from the eighteenth to
the sixteenth century BC.

The Early Minoan period still bore
many Neolithic features and was a
time of transition, as can be seen most
clearly in its pottery. In the early Middle
Minoan period - around 1900 BC
- the first palaces were built
at Knossos, Phaistos,
Mallia, Archanes, Za-
kros and Kydonia. It
is difficult to identify
the factors which
led to the concentra-
tion of power in royal
hands and to the founding of these
huge palace complexes, which
played their part in the rapid development of civilisation. At this
time, a new social, religious and e-
conomic organisation came into being. The system of government
seems to have been theocratic, and
society itself to have consisted of a
number of classes. The palaces were
not simply administrative and religious centres, but also places where
products were turned out to meet the
needs of the Cretans and also for ex-
port. There was extensive trade with
Cyprus, Egypt and Syria, and colonies
such as those of Milos and Kythira
were founded. Trade - which
flourished at this time -
was under royal con-
trol, and there was a

p. 13

*Clay figurine of
the Old Palace
period (1900-
1700 BC) in the
form of an armed
man in an
attitude of worship.
Found at the
mountain-top
sanctuary at
Petsofa. (Irakleio
Archaeological
Museum)*

well-organised fleet to ensure that Crete ruled the waves and that pirates could not raid its coasts. The Minoan thalassocracy reached the height of its powers, and art of the finest quality was produced in Crete. Around 1700 BC, however, a violent earthquake shook the island and damaged the palaces, which were soon completely destroyed by fire. We do not know whether this disaster was the work of the forces of nature alone, or whether there was also an invasion. The palaces were soon rebuilt, still larger and more magnificent than before, and the Late Palace period now began: this period, lasting from 1700 BC to 1400 BC, was the most brilliant of the Minoan civilisation. Mallia, Zakros, Phaistos and above all Knossos were never more splendid. Thanks to its central position, Knossos was able to unify the entire island, construct a good network of roads and serve as an economic and political leader. The economic life of the island flourished

p. 14

Restored western porch of the northern entrance corridor. The northern cistern can be seen in the background.

at this time, there was a wealth of farming and stock-breeding production and much produce was exported to mainland Greece and the surrounding islands. The royal families, the nobility and the officials of state exploited most of the land, and only small holdings of fertile ground were left for ordinary people - most of them craftsmen employed in the palaces. Many Minoans worked on the ships which enabled the kings to profit from trade. Various systems of writing were used, including the hieroglyphic system (similar to that of Egypt, with each letter represented by a depiction or an animal or object) and the syllabic script known as Linear A, consisting of simplified shapes but as yet undeciphered. After 1450 BC, when Achaean power came to Crete, Linear B script was introduced. Around 1400 BC, at the time when Minoan civilisation was at its zenith, earthquakes and fires wrecked Knossos and the other palaces and emptied the cities. This cata-

p. 16 -17 ➤

Minoan wall-painting from Knossos, showing bull-leaping. (Irakleio Archaeological Museum)

p. 15

View of the western storehouses with their storage jars. Among the jars, rows of square tanks which were lined with alabaster plaques can be seen.

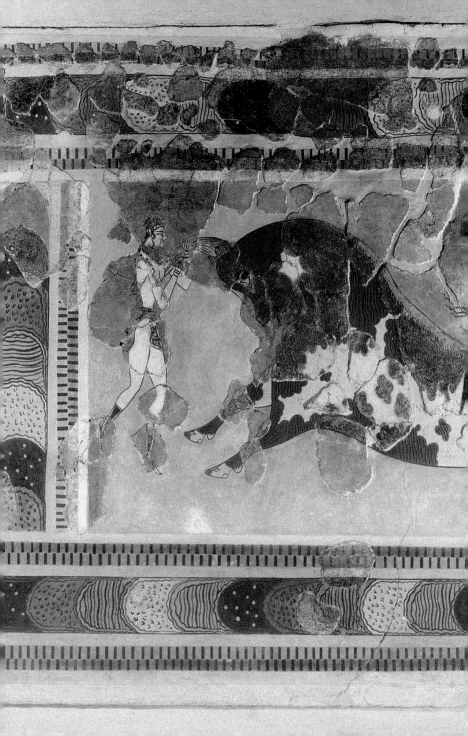

strophe may have been the result of a volcanic erup-
tion on Santorini. On the other hand, the discovery of
part of the palace archives written in Linear B (that is,
in the same script as that found in the Mycenean
palaces) might lead us to the hypothesis that the Minoan civilisation was overwhelmed by foreign invasion. However the case may be, the palace of Knossos
was completely destroyed at this time and Crete as a
whole went into a gradual decline which led down to
the Dorian invasion of around 1100 BC.

Art, Life and Religion in Minoan Crete

Minoan art is divided into three periods: Early Minoan
(3600-2100 BC), Middle Minoan (2100-1600 BC) and
Late Minoan (1600-1200 BC). The golden age of Minoan art was that of the last of the three periods. The
Greek archaeologist Nikolaos Platon, however, used
historical events to produce a different chronological
division of Minoan art into the Prepalatial, Protopala-
tial and Neopalatial periods.

Thanks to their love of elegance and beauty, the Minoans were able to score successes in many fields of
art. Their artworks - usually small in size - stand out
for their grace, originality and vitality. Architecture was
a sphere of particular achievement, with the four great
palaces of Knossos, Phaistos, Zakros and Mallia as the
outstanding examples. The architecture of Minoan
tombs is interesting too: apart from burials in caves
and on the coast, they also interred their dead in
vaulted and rock tombs. Yet their greatest love of
all was painting, in which the basic thematic ele-
ments were the human body and motifs from the
plant and animal kingdom. In the Neopalatial period, Minoan wall-painting reached its zenith - always in close connection with architecture and
adapted to the functional needs of the rooms being decorated. The palace wall-paintings show
scenes from everyday life and religious cere-

◄ *p. 18*

*Detail from a wall-
painting of a religious
ceremony, showing
the beautiful priestess
known as the
'Parisian'. Found in
the palace of Knossos
and dating from
1500-1450 BC.
(Irakleio Archaeological
Museum)*

p. 19

*Faience plaque,
showing the facade of
a three-storey house.*

p. 21 ►

The 'Snake Goddess' - a famous figurine of faience showing the goddess of fertility wearing an elaborate costume. 1600-1580 BC. (Irakleio Archaeological Museum)

p. 20

The 'Harvester Vase' (1550-1500 BC). It shows men returning from work in the fields. Found at Ayia Triada. (Irakleio Archaeological Museum)

monies. Landscapes were popular too, along with sea scenes such as the famous 'Dolphin' wall-painting. In many of these paintings there is a predominant sense of movement, and some of the most interesting contain very many characters. Among the best-known paintings are the 'Parisienne' (a religious rite being conducted by a beautiful priestess), the 'Prince with the Lilies', and the scene showing the 'bull-leaping' (the ritual bullfight of the ancient Minoans, connected with the worship of the sacred bull). Wall-painting had a direct impact on the painting of vases, which gradually lost its purely ornamental character and began to incorporate themes from nature adjusted to the curving surface of the vase. Sculpture was much less highly developed than painting: in Crete we find neither monumental sculptures nor cult statues, but only small figurines. In the important vases and other pottery of Minoan Crete, we can see the love of colour that distinguished these early people. The delicate vases of what is known as Kamares ware (given that name from the fact that the first find of such pottery was in a cave at Kamares) are particularly rich in colour, and were exported throughout the Mediterranean. In the final phase of the palace at Knossos, an order of pottery was introduced which relied on the principles of symmetry and rhythmicality. The themes of the paintings on these vases did not change, but the shapes became more schematic. Evans named pottery of this kind 'palace ware'. However, it was in small-scale works of art that the Cretan genius excelled. They were wonderful workers in stone, where their

65

refined techniques enabled them to combine harder and softer stones in creating utensils of great beauty and boldness. Of particular interest are the Minoan rhytons, vases made out of black steatite. In their miniature sculptures and utensils, the Minoans made use of a wide range of types of stone together with more sensitive materials such as ivory and faience. Their metal objects, too - such as the votive offerings found in sanctuaries and caves - are often works of art. The gold jewellery of the age (most of the surviving examples of which come from burials) was unsurpassed. In many cases, the core of the jewellery was bronze, covered with pressed or hammered gold leaf.

p. 22

Typical Minoan objects in gold are the double axes, religious symbols, such as those shown here, from the Arkalochori Cave.

The scenes shown on these various works of art have much to tell us about the way people lived in those distant times. Society continued to be organised on a theocratic basis - indeed, as the final phase of Mi-

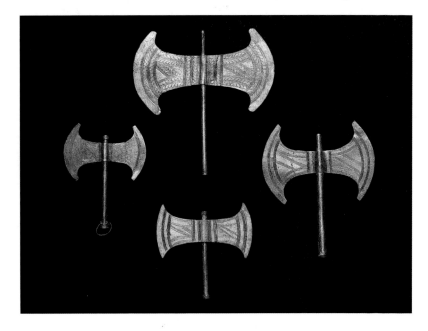

noan civilisation began, this feature became even more intense. The king was also the chief priest, and it may be that the name 'Minos' had some religious significance. The Minoans were members of a Mediterranean race. They were of moderate height and slight build, with dark hair, eyes and skin. The men dressed lightly, wearing only a length of colourful cloth round the waist, while officials had cloaks and head-bands. Both sexes wore tight belts to accentuate the waist. Fashion for women in Minoan Crete dictated the wearing of an open-fronted bodice (the bosom was sometimes covered with transparent material) and wide skirts with pleats, frills and panels. The hair was combed in various elaborate ways, sometimes with curls hanging down over the forehead, and a wide range of headgear was worn. The women of Minoan Crete were emancipated, with their

p. 23

Pendant from a necklace of the Neopalatial period (1700-1450 BC), showing two bees storing honey in a honeycomb. (Irakleio Archaeological Museum)

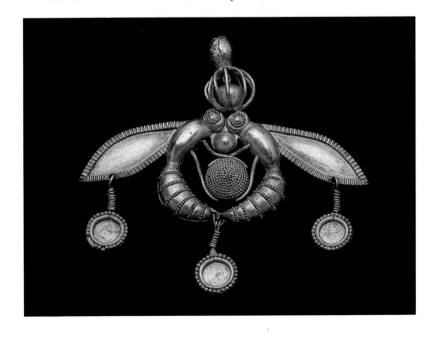

own special position in society. The paintings of the time show them attending religious ceremonies with the menfolk, or watching public meetings, dances and sporting contests. The short, slim and agile Minoans were pleasure-loving and had little time for the art of war - thus explaining the rarity of fighting or hunting scenes in Minoan art. The cult of the bull and the feasts and games connected with it (bull-leaping and bullfighting) was associated with the spring, the time of the year when nature was reborn and man with it. Each year, the priest caste of the Minoan religion - headed by the king of Knossos - held rites and sacrifices. The bull was associated with fertility and deemed to be sacred (Zeus transformed himself into a bull on a number of occasions); other sacred symbols were the snake, the double horns, the double axe, the sacred knot, the octagonal shield, and the sacred tree. Particular importance was attached to the female deity associated with fertility and eternal life, who was worshipped in special sanctuaries laid out in caves and on mountain tops. The Cretans seem to have believed in life after death, burying their dead with great ceremony and accompanying them with vessels of food and other useful everyday things. The corpse was placed on a wooden stretcher or in a sarcophagus made of wood, stone or clay, with items that the dead person had loved or might find useful in the afterlife being placed around it.

p. 25 ▶

Above: 'The Blue Ladies' - wall-painting of women, c.1600 BC, found in Wing A of the Knossos palace and on show in the Irakleio Museum.

Below: The famous stone sarcophagus from Ayia Triada, dating from 1400 BC. Its fine decoration is a basic source of information on the religious and cult rituals of the period. (Irakleio Archaeological Museum)

From the Geometric Period to Helleno-Roman Times (1100 BC - 330 AD)

In around 900 BC, not long after their arrival from mainland Greece, the Dorian invaders of Crete organised themselves into city-states and compelled the descendants of the Minoans to retreat into the mountains. The Dorians brought new customs and practices with them (such as the burning of the dead and the stan-

dard Greek pantheon), and they also introduced the use of iron. The Doric cities imitated the system of government implemented in Sparta - that is, rule by a kind of senate of noblemen. In general, life was organised along the lines traditionally thought of as 'Spartan', with pervasive military discipline. Rule by the aristocrats attached great importance to legislation, as we can see from the legal text on the famous Gortyn inscription of the sixth century BC (discovered in 1884). These city-states formed a union under the leadership of Knossos when it came to repelling attack from outside. They were fortified, each having walls and an acropolis for safety in times of conflict with other cities on the island or of raids from mainland Greece and the coast of Asia. However, the fundamental disunity of the Doric cities caused trade to fall away, and Crete declined little by little.

In the **Classical period**, Crete was cut off from the rest of Greece. It took no part in the Persian Wars and remained neutral throughout the Peloponnesian War, largely because the strife between the cities of the island (and their rival alliances) left little scope for military involvement elsewhere. Naturally enough, art could not flourish in such circumstances, and so such Classical sculptures as have survived are few in number and provincial in character. Civil war among the city-states continued unabated through the **Hellenistic period**. At this time, though, the cities of Crete began to form broader alliances with one another and with the Greek kings of other lands, thus fostering the constant interference of third parties in the island's affairs. In this period, too, art was imitative and provincial.

Rome began to intervene in Cretan affairs as early as the second century BC. At this time, however, it confined itself to acting as mediator, given that it had its own problems and civil wars. The Cretans had joined with the pirates of Cilicia in raiding Roman ports and terrorising shipping - and they had also formed an alliance with King Mithridates of Pont, a sworn enemy of Rome. The two events combined to turn Roman wrath on Crete. Mark Antony was the first commander sent against the island, but the combined Cretan forces drove him off. Eventually - in 67 BC, after three years of bitter fighting - the island fell to Metellus, who surnamed himself Creticus to mark his triumph, and became a province of the Roman Empire with Knossos, and later Gortyn, as its capital. The civilisation of Crete was strongly influenced by that of Rome, although it never lost its own special character. Greek continued to be the language of the people, with Latin being used only for administrative purposes. At this time, Christianity came to Crete and was spread by Titus, a disciple of St Paul. Although the Cretan economy was plunged into disarray by the temporary suspension of piracy and reduced demand for mercenaries, in-

p. 27

The Odeion of ancient Gortyn.

creased trade soon improved the situation. The Romans put up many important public buildings and also constructed new roads to link the cities of the island and promote trade.

The Byzantine Period (330 - 1204)

Throughout the centuries of Byzantine rule, Crete continued to be a place of strategic importance for trade in the Mediterranean. The Byzantine history of the island falls into two phases. In the first, from 330 to 826, Crete enjoyed considerable prosperity. In 330, the island ceased to be a part of the province of Cyrenacia and was incorporated into that of Illyria - and after the split in the Roman Empire in the reign of Theodosius the Great (395) it joined the Eastern Roman Empire. The capital of what was now a Byzantine province was at Gortyn, and Crete was administered by a *consularius* appointed by the Emperor himself. Later, from the fifth to the ninth century, Crete constituted a separate 'theme' (province) of the Empire. In the mid-seventh century, however, it became the target of increasingly frequent raids on the part of the Arabs based in North Africa and Syria. In 824 the Saracens conquered Crete, which they made into an independent Arab state with its capital at Handak, the city now called Herakleio, round which they dug a deep moat. 'Handak' is an Arabic word, and it means 'ditch'. Under the Arabs, Christianity was persecuted and lost some of its grip: the churches of Crete were demolished or converted into mosques, and the Cretans were forcibly converted to Islam. The Byzantines tried repeatedly - but in vain - to recapture the island, and it was not until 961, after an Arab occupation lasting 137 years, that Nicephorus Phocas, a superb general and later Emperor, succeeded in liberating Crete. Even then, he had to deploy a huge fleet and a vast army, and the siege of Handak lasted many months. Once Crete was back in the Byzantine Empire, Christianity revived and the island economy began to recover. Conditions were now suitable for some centuries of peaceful development and renewed cultural growth.

Venetian Rule (1204 - 1669)

The second period of Byzantine rule came to an end in 1204, when the Empire was (temporarily) overthrown by the Crusaders. In the division of the spoils that followed, Crete passed into the hands of Boniface of Monserrat, who decided to make his home in Thessaloniki and sold the island to the Venetians for 1,000 pieces of silver and some concessions. But before the Venetians could land, Genoese pirates under Enrico Pescatore, Count of Malta, occupied Crete. They built castles in strategic places and repaired the walls of Handak, which enabled them to hold out against the Venetians until 1212. The Cretan reaction to this imposition of foreign rule took the form of one revolt af-

p. 29

The Frankocastello Venetian fortress stands almost at the water's edge. Rectangular in shape, it has square towers at each corner.

p. 31 ▶

The Venetian lighthouse is an adornment to Chania's harbour and a monument to the Venetian presence in the city and the island generally.

p. 30

View of the Loggia, the meeting-place of the nobles under Venetian rule. Today it houses Irakleio's Town Hall.

ter another. For a short time they succeeded in liberating themselves and in declaring Crete the independent 'Republic of St Tito', but the Venetians were back before long. Under the new conqueror, Crete was divided into three and later four administrative provinces, where the authorities resided in the main towns, and a much larger number of districts (castellanies), where there were powerful Venetian fortresses. Herakleio was renamed Candia - a corruption of the earlier (and Byzantine) nomenclature of Handak - and remained capital of the whole island. The walls of Herakleio were built at this time, along with numerous superb edifices, such as the palace of the Doge, the basilica of St Mark and the Loggia, where the Venetian nobility congregated. When Constantinople fell to the Turks in 1453, many Greek aristocrats and intellectuals took refuge in Venetian Crete, thus contributing to the flourishing there of what was now post-Byzantine art and learning. A new school of painting came into being: that called the 'Cretan school', which combined influences from Byzantine and Italian Renaissance art. The main representatives of the Cretan School were Michail Damaskinos, Klontzas and Ioannis Cornaros. Literature, too, flourished during the closing years of Venetian rule. Among the most important works are the *Erophile* and the *Panoria* of Georgios Hortatzis, the *Sacrifice* of Abraham of Vincenzo Cornaros and, of course, the same author's epic poem *Erotocritos*. This outstanding work, written in around 1645 when the Turkish-

Venetian war was just beginning, is the story of the adventures of the princess Aretusa, daughter of King Herakles of Athens, and of Erotocritos, son of the courtier Pezostratos. For over three hundred years now, generations of Greeks have been reared on the ten thousand lines of this superb blend of epic and lyric poetry. Songs, dirges and theatrical works have been quarried out of Erotocritos, and it has kept its place in the hearts of all the Greeks - though of the Cretans in particular, who approach it with true passion.

Turkish Rule (1669-1898)

In 1645, a huge force of invading Turks managed to land to the west of Chania and occupy the islet of Thodorou. The Turks then laid close siege to the city of Chania, which put up a stout fight but was compelled to surrender. Rethymno held out for a further two months, but within three years - by late 1648 - all the island except Candia was in Turkish hands.

The siege of Candia (the 'Great Castle') became legendary: the Cretan capital resisted the besiegers for 21 whole years, writing as it did so one of the most glorious chapters in the modern history of the island. In the end, however, on 27 September 1669 the city was forced to sue for peace when one of its Venetian defenders turned traitor and revealed the weak points in the fortifications to the Turks. The Venetians were allowed to sail away on their own ships, taking with them their religious treasures and such of their goods as they could carry. Crete was left to pay the heavy price of the hopeless Venetian struggle: crushing taxation, confiscation of public and private property (which passed into the hands of mosques, Muslim charities, pashas, beys and agas), theft, murder, torture and compulsory conversion to Islam. Many Christians were obliged to keep their faith secret, while others took refuge in the Venetian castles or in the mountains. The Turkish occupation had a disastrous impact on Crete. The population fell dramatically as a result of the lengthy Turkish-Venetian war and the mass exiling of sections of the population, especially from the urban centres. Forced conversion to Islam played its part here, too. The economy regressed to primitive forms of farming and stock-breeding, while trade dwindled away to almost nothing. Of course, organised resistance to the conquerors was not long in coming, sometimes receiving the assistance of the Venetians (1692) and sometimes encouraged by the Russians (the Daskaloyannis rising in Sfakia, 1770).

The Greek War of Independence which broke out in 1821 found Crete only too ready and willing to fight for its freedom. The battles lasted for almost ten years, with many rapid reverses of fortune: great successes, but bitter defeats, too. The campaigning in Crete can be divided into two phases: during the first, lasting to 1824, the Ottoman Empire summoned large forces of Egyptians to the island and succeeded in defeating the rebels in a series of murderous battles. However, the revolt broke out again at Gramvousa in 1825, spread throughout the island and kept itself alive until 1830. But the London Protocol of 22 January 1830 dashed all the hopes that nearly ten years of bloody fighting had raised by leaving Crete outside the frontiers of the new and independent Greek state and placing absolute power in the hands of the Sultan. Later, Sultan Mahmud IV conceded Crete to Mehmet Ali, Viceroy of Egypt. The crisis in the Eastern Question which broke out in 1839-40 and Mehmet Ali's defeat in Syria seriously weakened Egyptian power in Crete. The Great Powers detached the island from Egypt and brought it back under the rule of the Sultan. Throughout this period, the Cretans kept up their struggle for liberty, placing their hopes in the Greek state and the Great Powers and employing, alternately, their weapons

p. 34 - 35 ▶

View of the harbour of Irakleio, where the imposing presence of the Venetian fortress (Koules) reminds visitors of the history of the town.

and their diplomatic skills in the step-by-step approach to freedom. There were risings in 1841, in 1858 - which resulted in a temporary improvement in conditions on the island - and in 1866, when the islanders received unofficial aid from Greece. The last of these rebellions, which was the ultimate expression of the Cretan passion for freedom and unification with Greece, lasted almost three years, until 1869, and during it many notable acts of heroism and self-sacrifice took place. The struggle culminated in the holocaust

The Isle of CANDI

Published Dec.ʳ 29, 1781, by I.

of the besieged monastery of Arkadi, after which the
Great Powers brought pressure on Turkey to cede an
'organic law' under which Crete became a General
Administration whose commander was assisted by
Muslim and Christian deputies.

Needless to say, the Turks found various pretexts
for violating these agreements. A fresh rising led to the
Halepa Pact of 1878, under which the Christian population of Crete was granted self-government. The last
act in the Cretan tragedy was the massacre of Herak-

p. 36 - 37

*Engraving (Museum
Benaki -Athens)*

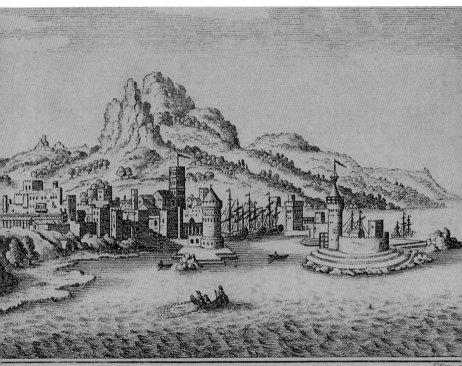

ı the Mediterranean.

ding N.º23, Paternoster Row.

leio of 25 August 1898, soon after which the last Turkish troops left the island. The liberation of Crete was eventually a fact.

Recent History: 1898 to the Present Day

In 1898, with the help of the European Powers, Crete became an autonomous province under Prince George of Greece as governor. However, the struggle now became one for union with Greece and was to last for quite a few more years. It culminated in the Therisos rebellion of 1905, which led directly to the resignation of Prince George, the abolition of the position of governor and de facto union with Greece in 1908 - for which Eleftherios Venizelos was primarily responsible. Official unification with Greece did not take place until after the Balkan Wars of 1912-13, when the Treaty of London was signed on 17/30 May 1913.

The most recent occasion on which the Cretans displayed their heroism and self-sacrifice was during the Second World War. In May 1941, the airborne German attack on the island found Crete without Greek troops (who had been sent to the front in Albania) and with its Allied defenders ill-prepared for such an assault. The Battle of Crete, between highly-trained and fully-armed German paratroops on the one side and scratch units of Allied and Greek forces, poorly equipped but willing to sacrifice themselves, on the other, lasted ten days and brought the Germans to the brink of defeat. In the end, the might of the German military machine was victorious, but the Cretans continued their resistance throughout the Occupation period - and the fact that the Battle of Crete took place at all held up the German attack on Russia.

The end of the War was the conclusion of a long period when Crete had been continuously engaged in resisting occupying powers, and marked the start of a time of peace and reconstruction.

◄ *p. 38*

Portrait of Eleftherios Venizelos. Venizelos served seven times as Prime Minister of Greece and had a profound effect on the course of its modern history.

The Folk Art of Crete

The folk culture of Crete is among the most distinctive forms of vernacular art to be found in the Greek world. The feature which has had the greatest impact on that culture is the geographical position of the island. Crete, isolated at the southernmost extremity of the Greek world and poised at the crossroads between three continents, created and has maintained a local cultural tradition influenced by both East and West. A further impact on that culture came from the long and troubled history of the island and from its various conquerors - Arabs, Venetians and Turks. Yet despite these influences the folk culture of Crete is notable for its conservatism and its adherence to ancient and Byzantine models. Similarities can be seen between the implements and utensils used today and those of Minoan times, and even in the customs and religious practices of the islanders. The plough in use today is the same as that described by Hesiod, and storage jars of the Minoan type are still made. The dead are mourned in much the same manner as in Homer's time, and the first grapes of the year receive the same blessing.

Folk music is among the most characteristic features of Cretan culture. The artistic, poetic souls of the Cretans are reflected in their *mantinádes,* short songs in couplet form full of sweetness, passion and sentiment. The *mantinádes* of Crete are usually love-songs, but satirical versions are not uncommon - and a feature of all such songs is that they have to be composed extempore, as an answer to the couplet which has just been sung. This improvisation often takes the form of a poetic contest a-

p. 41 ▶

*Cretan girl
in traditional
embroidered costume.*

mong the singers, or between the singer and the player of the Cretan *lyra* (fiddle). Another form of song native to Crete is the *rizítika,* songs from the west of the island which take their generic name because they were believed to originate in the villages of the foothills *(rizá)* of the White Mountains. Dances and songs are accompanied by the local musical instruments, the most characteristic of which is the Cretan *lyra,* a three-stringed wooden fiddle which, in the hands of a Cretan instrumentalist, expresses all the artistic soul of a people noted for their strength of personality. The *moirológia* (dirges) of Crete are yet another category of lyric poetry: these mournful

p. 42

The dynamic folk dances of Crete accompany every expression of the social life of its people.

songs over the dead are an ancient custom still widely observed, especially in mountain regions.

The traditional costume of the men of Crete combines severity and pride. It consists of the *vráka* (baggy trousers), the *meidanoyíleko* (a sleeveless waistcoat), a black shirt, a long crimson cummerbund, *stivánia* (tall leather boots) and a linen kerchief with bobbles covering the head.

Architecture

The conquerors of Crete - and the Venetians and Turks in particular - have left their mark on the architecture of

p. 43

Typical scenes from the farmers' life in Crete. A: Harvest. B: Winnowing. The cultivation of the soil of Crete requires hard and unremitting toil of its farmers, but the wealth of its produce is a fitting reward.

the island. The spacious, well-lit urban houses and mansions of the cities of Venetian Crete, with their large windows, sculpted ornamentation and elaborate facades, displayed the spirit of the Renaissance and differed greatly from the contemporaneous buildings of mainland Greece under the Turks, where houses were fortified like towers and turned a closed, unarticulated face on the world. At this time, the cities of Crete also had public squares, fountains, loggias and clock-towers. The walls of Candia were built under the Venetians - a process that took a whole century - as were those of Rethymno and Chania, and fortresses (castelli) rose on spots of strategic importance such as Spinalonga and Frangokastello.

After the fall of Crete to the Turks (1669), the Renaissance style became less frequent in architecture and was replaced by a type of housing much more reminiscent of the 'tower-houses' of the mainland. The facades of the houses of Turkish-occupied Crete were severe and flat, with tall, narrow windows and almost no ornamentation. Yet despite the fact that Renaissance forms in architecture became less common and the introduction of a more enclosed and severe type, some decorative motifs managed to survive, though in a more schematic and simplified form.

The earliest and simplest type of village house consisted of one floor only - indeed, of one room. There were also more complex types with two floors: here the ground floor served as a stable and barn (and sometimes a shop), while the upper floor was the living quarters for the family. Here would be the reception room (the *piano nobile*), the bedrooms and service areas. One of the principal characteristics of such houses was that they always had flat roofs of beaten earth. The *kamaróspito* ('arch-

p. 44

Inside, the ordinary houses are austerely plain. The only decoration is provided by the few items of furniture, which are, however, masterpieces of woodcarving, and the rich natural colours of the produce of the soil of Crete.

p. 45

Above: Reconstruction of the interior of a traditional Cretan house. An important place is occupied by the loom on which the textiles for which Crete is famous are made. (Historical Museum of Crete, Room 10)

Below: A: Exterior of an ordinary farmer's house.

B: Exterior of a Cretan house, with the typical enclosed balcony.

house') was another type of residence, articulated around a stone-built semi-circular arch.

Inside, the Cretan house had little furniture, and the predominant feature was the *pezoúla*, a raised stone platform which served as a bed. There might also be a sofás, a kind of attic used as sleeping quarters. Movable furniture was confined to a couch (or a drawing-room suite in wealthier establishments), a table, a chest for the safe-keeping of valuable clothes and the trousseau of the lady of the house, and some chairs. There would also be a *teláro* (loom). There may not have been much furniture, but each piece was a masterpiece of wood-carving.

p. 46

A woodcarver employs his instinctive aesthetic sense and many years of experience to produce the traditional wooden spoons, an art which lives on in Crete.

Folk art

The Cretans bring authentic artistic talent and great enthusiasm to bear in their production of art-works. They distinguish themselves particularly in the fields of wood-carving, folk music instruments, knife-making, basket-

weaving, and pottery, while the women weave cloth and embroider. The woven goods of Crete are famous throughout Greece for the variety and vividness of their colours and designs. Among the most representative products of the weavers of Crete are *pataniés* (bed-covers with striking combinations of design and colour), cummerbunds for the male costume, *druvádes* (bags in a single colour or a number of shades) and tablecloths.

Crete has a long tradition in pottery-making. The most important villages for this craft are Kentri (near Ierapetra), Margarites (near Rethymno), Halepa (near Chania), and, above all, Thrapsano near Herakleio, where the tradition of pottery has been alive for 4,000 years and where pots and vases in the Minoan style are still made. The making of knives is important, too; the knife was an essential part of the male costume (and often of the female costume, too) and this led to demand capable of supporting knife foundries in Chania and Herakleio. Over time, the knife ceased to be a weapon and is now mere-

p. 47

The women of Crete continue to make high-quality textiles in attractive patterns and colours, a result of their great skill in using the traditional loom.

ly a supplement and ornament to the male costume. Coins usually hang from its handle, and the blade will have *mantinádes* incised on it.

Cretan cooking

The traditional diet of the people of Crete is simple and austere, based on the bread which is kept in huge baskets. Religious, social and magical beliefs or superstitions lay behind the decorated bread which is made on special occasions with great ceremony and which constitutes an unusual form of artistic expression. Such bread is made at Christmas time (when it is called *christópsomo* or *stavrópsomo)*, at Easter *(avgokouloúres,* topped with eggs, and *lambrokouloúres)* and for the feast of Our Lady on 15 August *(ftázyma)*. Special bread is also baked for weddings and christenings (that of Anogeia being particularly prized). The decoration on the bread is made with pieces of dough in relief, and constitutes an interesting form of folk art. Another notable product of the baker's art are *kalitsoúnia*, little

p. 48

Interior of a traditional bakery which makes the famous Cretan rusks, decorative loaves and a host of other delicacies.

hand-made patties filled with cream cheese *(anthótyro),* and Cretan pancakes *(xerotígana).*

The basic products of the soil of Crete are olives (and their oil) and grapes (from which wine and raisins are made). Salad greens are cultivated and picked wild; these can be simply boiled or made into dishes such as *sofeyáda,* a favourite summer dish in which cultivated greens of various kinds are cooked with plenty of olive oil and tomatoes. The Cretans are great eaters of snacks, including snails (which are cooked *bourbouristí:* fried with olive oil and salt) and mushrooms (also fried). Meat is also common, and is cooked in various ways. The killing of the family pig at Christmas time provides a wide variety of foodstuffs: sausages, brawn, and *omathiés,* a preparation in which the intestine of the animal is stuffed with its innards, rice, raisins and spices. Large pieces of lamb or goat are roasted over a charcoal grill (the *koftó* method). *Stáka* is made from butter and flour, and the *Sfakia toúrta* involves oven-roasting lamb wrapped in pastry with *myzíthra* cheese. The most popular drinks are authentic Cretan wine and *rakí* or *tsikoudiá,* a powerful spirit. Rakí can be distilled from mulberries *(mournóraki),* and this is often used as rubbing alcohol in folk medicine. The *Kazanémata -* the days during which the *rakí* is distilled - are an opportunity for feasting, dancing and singing. Tavernas and cook-shops are to be found all over Crete, and provide a hospitable and simple environment in which the traditional food and drink of Crete can be enjoyed.

p. 49

The famous Cretan raki is still produced in the traditional manner. The days when it is made have a festal character in Crete and are called 'Kazanémata'.

The Terrain and Natural Environment

Crete is the largest island in Greece, accounting for the fact that the Greeks often refer to it as *Megalónisos,* the 'big island'. Its area of 8,261 square kilometres also makes it the fifth-largest island in the Mediterranean. Crete lies in the south of the Aegean Sea, in the centre of the East Mediterranean basin, at the point where Europe, Asia and Africa meet. It is orientated east-west and is a long and narrow island, thus explaining its ancient name of *Dolichí* (long). On the north coast there are large bays and sandy beaches, while on the south - the side facing the Libyan Sea - the indentations of the coastline are much smaller. Souda Bay, on the north coast, is the largest natural harbour. There are a number of islets - Ayii Theodori, Ayii Pantes, Spinalonga, Pseira and Gavdos to the south, all uninhabited save the last - scattered around its coast. Gavdos has been identified with Calpyso's island in the *Odyssey.*

p. 51 ▶

A typical view of the Cretan landscape with its high mountains and wild vegetation.

The terrain of Crete is very variable. In the west, orange groves alternate with mountain plateaus, and in eastern Crete palm trees interrupt verdant mountain slopes on which olives and vines grow. Yet most of Crete is mountainous, with three major mountain ranges - the White Mountains, Mt Ida (or Psiloritis) and Mt Diktis (or the Lasithi Mountains) - crossing the entire island and rising to heights of 2,500 metres. There are mountain plateaus high among the sum-

mits, fertile plains (especially in the south) and numerous gorges. Rivers are short and few in number, and there is only one lake - Lake Kourna - beautifully situated in the Prefecture of Chania (subprefecture of Apokoronou). Crete also has a wealth of caves. Most of them have been known since Neolithic times, when they were used as human habitations and as religious sanctuaries. The Diktaean Cave and the Idaean Cave are the most important caverns. The climate of Crete varies sharply from the mountains down to the coast via the plains. In general, however, the climate is Mediterranean - indeed, it is the mildest and healthiest to be found anywhere in Europe. Thanks to this variety of natural and climatological features, Crete has an unusually wide range of agricultural products, many of them cultivated all year round. The island produces olives, grapes, citrus fruit, aromatic and medicinal herbs, garden

p. 52

Striking landscape from the plateau of Lasithi with its famous windmills.

produce, bananas, avocados and kiwi fruit. There are extensive forests, and flowers, bushes and herbs grow in abundance - including Cretan dittany *(Origanum dictamus)*, whose medicinal powers have been known since ancient times. The fauna of Crete is rich, too, and can boast a unique species of wild goat (locally known as the *kri-kri* or *agrími*), which lives in the Samaria Gorge, the ravines of the White Mountains and on the surrounding islets. Stock-breeding and fishing play an important part in life on Crete. Sheep and goats are bred, and dairy products of exceptional quality - *graviéra* (the Greek *Gruyère)*, *anthótyros* and *myzíthra* - are easy to find. With a population of over 500,000 (at the 1981 census), Crete is one of the ten Greek regions. It consists of four Prefectures: those of Chania (with its capital at Chania), Rethymno (Rethymno), Herakleio (Herakleio) and Lasithi (Ayios Nikolaos).

p. 53

Above: The fine beach at Preveli attracts a host of visitors every year.

Below: View of the famous palm trees of Vaï.

1. The Prefecture of Chania

This is the most westerly prefecture of Crete, with towering mountain massifs, deep gorges and a coastline with both steep cliffs and fine beaches. In the north of the Prefecture is the large plain of Chania, with the White Mountains on three sides of it. Apart from its natural beauties, the Prefecture of Chania also has numerous archaeological sites and other places connected with history. The area of the Prefecture is 2,375 square kilometres. Its capital is Chania, and it is divided into five subprefectures: Kydonia, Apokoronou, Kissamos, Selino and Sfakia. The islets of Gavdos and Gavdopoula, far out in the Libyan Sea, also belong to the Prefecture of Chania.

Chania

Chania, capital of the Prefecture of the same name, has a population of 60,000. It stands on the neck of a small promontory on the east side of Chania Bay. The visitor's first impression of the constantly growing modern city is a good one: this is a well-planned town, with broad streets, parks, pedestrian precincts, tasteful buildings. This picture is supplemented by well-preserved neo-Classical buildings, the covered market and whatever has remained of the Venetian and Turkish periods of the history of Chania, and completed with the flowers and green open spaces to be found everywhere in the centre and the suburbs. Indeed, Chania has been called 'the city of flowers'. Chania is a modern coastal city with a full range of tourist facil-

p. 55 ▶

View of Chania's picturesque harbour. The building with domes, next to the busy tavernas and cafés, was once a Turkish mosque and now houses the offices of the National Tourist Organisation of Greece.

ities. It has abundant hotels of all categories, together with boarding-houses and hostels capable of accomodating a large number of visitors. There are plenty of restaurants, tavernas, fish tavernas, ouzo bars, patisseries, cafes, bars, discos, and night-clubs where local music can be enjoyed.

p. 56

Chania has its own narrow alleyways where a walk among buildings in the traditional style is an enjoyable experience.

History

Chania stands on the site of the ancient city of Cydonia: archaeological excavations on Kastelli hill have brought to light a Minoan settlement with a building of the megaron type. Tombs of the Minoan or Late Minoan period have been found all over the town. Ancient Cydonia flourished throughout the Roman period. Under the Arabs it was renamed Al Hanim - of which 'Chania' is a corruption - and under the second period of Byzantine rule it went into decline. In 1252, the Venetians effectively rebuilt it in accordance with Western urban planning models, later adding fortifications to keep out pirates. They also rebuilt the castle (Kastelli), where the governor had his palace and which was the location of the Catholic church and the houses of the Venetian officials. At this time, Chania became a place of considerable commercial and economic importance, sometimes being called the 'Venice of the East'. In 1645

it was taken by the Turks, although they were never fully in control of the hinterland. In the period of Ottoman rule, Chania was the seat of a pasha, and after 1850 the castle of Chania housed the administration of the entire island. After the proclamation of Cretan autonomy in 1897, the Turks left and Chania became the capital of the independent state. It was also the seat of the High Commissioner. The seal was set on the union of Crete with Greece when the Greek flag was raised over the castle (1 December 1913). The Battle of Crete began near Chania (at Malame and Galata) in 1941. Military operations centred around Chania, and the city later became a focus for the resistance movement.

Tour of the town

Chania consists of the Old and New Towns, which blend into a harmonious whole. The Old Town is the historic centre of the city, and all its buildings are scheduled for preservation. There are five quarters, without any distinct dividing lines between them: Top Hana (or Topanas), Ovraiki, Syntrivani, Splantza (Plaza) and Kastelli. Narrow alleyways twist in and out among Venetian and Turkish buildings - signs of the conquerors who once ruled over this place. The Old Town is surrounded by fifteenth-century Venetian walls which are a good example of the military architecture of the time. There are also sections of medieval wall which have been incorporated into later buildings. **Topanas** is the westernmost part of the Old Town, and it has Venetian mansions lining medieval lanes. Under the Turks, this was the aristocratic Christian quarter, and the Great Powers had their consulates here. The name is of Turkish origin, coming from the tópia or cannon in the San Salvatore bastion. The northernmost part of the area, at the entrance to the harbour, is occupied by the **Firkas Fortress**, built in 1629. This was where the Greek flag was first raised in

1913 to mark the island's union with Greece. Now the Fortress houses the **Chania Maritime Museum** and there is an open-air theatre. Over the entrance towers a **Venetian lighthouse**, built in the sixteenth century. To the south of Topanas and to the left of the large Venetian **church of St Francis** - which now houses the **Archaeological Museum** - is the **Jewish Quarter** (Ovriaki). To the south of this area is the Schiavo or Lando Bastion, together with a section of wall. The old quarter of **Syntrivani** centres around **Eleftheriou Venizelou Square**, which was the heart of Chania at the time when Crete was independent. All the pioneers of art and intellectual life in early twentieth-century Crete met here. Around stand some old buildings, including the **Mosque of Hasan Pasha**, an Arab building which now houses the municipal information bureau, and the **Harbour Kiosk**, on the site of the old customs house. The **Kastelli quarter**, on the east side

p. 58

Part of Chania harbour. The morning light brings out the individual features of the houses and shops.

of the harbour, was the acropolis of ancient Cydonia. In 1252, the Venetians used the site to build their Castel Vecchio, perhaps because some sort of Byzantine fortress was already in position there. The palazzo of the Venetian governor of Chania stood on the highest point. Later, under the Turks, the pashas had their quarters there. Today, none of the buildings in this district has survived with the exception of the north side of the wall. The **Splantza** or **Plaza** quarter is to the north-east of Chania, close to Kastelli and the harbour with its boat-sheds built by the Venetians in the late fifteenth century. Today, nine of the twenty three arches under which ships were once repaired have survived. The square in this part of town is dominated by the **Church of St Nicholas**, once a part of a Dominican monastery, which the Turks converted into the Mosque of Sultan Ibrahim. Behind the church is the little Venetian chapel of **St Rocco**, with the **Church of**

p. 59

The imposing Arsenal (shipyards) near the harbour. Built by the Venetians in the late fifteenth century, of the original 23 vaults, only nine remain today.

Above: Interior of a typical bootmaker's. Even today, footwear here is hand-made in the traditional way.

Below: View of the Municipal Market of Chania.

Sts Cosmas and Damien a little further on. This was a Turkish quarter under Ottoman rule. Among the parts of the town which sprang up outside the old walls, the best-known districts are **Kum Kapi** (the name means 'sea gate'), the attractive and historic district of **Halepa**, **Kainourgia Chora** and **Bolari**.

Museums

The **Archaeological Museum** of Chania, housed in the Church of St Francis (21 Halidon St, tel. no. 0821-20334), has a fine collection of finds dating from Neolithic times to the Roman period, all from the Chania area and western Crete.

The **Historical Archive** and the **Museum of Crete** are in a neo-Classical building at 20 Sfakianaki St (tel. no. 22606); they have on show various objects and collections of historical interest, and the archives and personal effects of Eleftherios Venizelos.

p. 61

In Chania, the vistor can take a horse-drawn carriage to explore the streets and discover the attractions of the city.

p. 62

The central scene from the mosaic floor of the Roman 'House of Dionysus' of the third century AD at Chania. The subject is the discovery of Ariadne by Dionysus on Naxos. (Chania Archaeological Museum)

The **Folklore Museum**, in a hall which forms part of the Municipal Library (Kydonias Ave., tel. no. 23273), has collections of folk art, objects from everyday life and photographs.

The **Municipal Library** is located in the **Municipal Building** (Kydonias Ave., tel. no. 23273) and includes among its other important collections the personal library of Eleftherios Venizelos.

The **Maritime Museum** is in an old building belonging to the **Firkas Fortress** (tel. no. 26437); among its collections of items relating to the history of the Greek navy are models of ships from antiquity down to modern times.

p. 63 ►

Mosaic floor of a Roman house of the third century AD at Chania, depicting Neptune with Amymone. (Chania Archaeological Museum)

Trips starting from Chania

Shorter routes

1. Chrysopigi Monastery - Mournies - Koukounara mansion

After 3 km. along the road from Chania to Souda we come to a turning to the right which leads to the **Chrysopigi** (or Zoodochos Pigi, 'life-receiving spring') **Monastery**, consisting of a three-apsed church surrounded by a wall. If we continue to the west from the Chrysopigi Monastery (or return to Chania by the road along which we came and then head south), we will come, after 3.5 km., to the village of **Mournies**, where Eleftherios Venizelos was born. His simple stone-built house still stands there, with a collection of his personal effects in the form of a museum. The area around the village is densely planted with olive and citrus trees. Approximately 500 m. outside the village is **Agia Marina**, a cool oasis with plane trees, springs of running water and stone benches. Also near the village is the famous **Koukounara mansion**, a building in the Venetian style with gardens, fountains and the winged lion of St Mark. Nearby is the **monastery of St Eleutherius**, a seventeenth-century building of considerable architectural interest.

p. 67 ▶

A glimpse of everyday life in the mountains of Crete.

2. Chania - Therisos

We leave Chania in a westerly direction, for Kissamos, and soon come to a turning (left) through the village

of **Perivolia** to heroic **Therisos**. Part of our route leads through the imposing **Therisos gorge** or **gorge of Eleftherios Venizelos**, 6 km. in length. Two kilometres before we enter the village is the **Kato Sarakina** or **Elliniko** cave, which has produced archaeological finds showing that it was a place of worship in Neolithic and Minoan times. The historic village of Therisos stands among the foothills of the White Mountains at an altitude of 500 m. This place played an important part in the modern history of Crete, for its inhabitants never ceased to fight the Turks. The events of 1905, when Eleftherios Venizelos and his supporters here declared the outbreak of a rising that went down in history as the 'Therisos Rebellion', made the village more significant still. The rebellion was a protest over the totalitarian regime of Prince George which the Great Powers had imposed. The revolutionaries compelled Prince George to resign from his

p. 68

A fine beach with clean blue sea - one of many in the Prefecture of Chania.

post as High Commissioner and paved the way for u-
nion with Greece. In the village, the house which V-
enizelos used as his headquarters may be visited.

Longer routes

3. Chania - Platanias - Maleme - Tavronitis - Voukolies - Kantanos - Kakodiki - Palaiochora; return from Souyia via Rodovani - Temenia - Maralia - Epanochori - Ayia Eirini - Prases - Skines - Alikianos

p. 69

View of the seaside village of Ayia Marina, a well-organised resort with plenty of hotel accommodation.

We leave Chania in a westerly direction for Kissamos, and come first to the seaside village of **Ayii Apostoli**. A diversion from our route here will take us to

Galatas, famous as a scene of heroism and self-sacrifice during the fighting of the Second World War. The area is densely vegetated and has many streams; the beaches of **Kalamaki** and **Glaros** are the most popular in the vicinity. The coast road continues west through pretty villages such as **Kato Daratso**, **Ayia Marina**, **Kato Stalos** and **Platanias**. Next we come to **Maleme**, 16.5 km. to the west of Chania. The village was in the front line during the German attack of 1941, since the small aerodrome nearby was among the first targets of the paratroopers. After a total of 20 km. we come to **Tavronitis**, a village called after the river of the same name. A road here leads south to **Palaiochora**, while if we head straight on for Kastelli we will come to **Voukolies** (at an altitude of 110 m., on the west bank of the Tavronitis) and then **Floria** (at 580 m., the highest point on the route). After this point the road begins to descend in a southerly direction; after 58 km. we come to **Kantanos**, the chief town of the subprefecture of Selinos, in the midst of the fertile Selinos valley. The name 'Kantanos' means 'city of victory', and it comes from the town's long struggle for liberty. In the surrounding area are numerous Byzantine chapels with fine wall-paintings. We continue through **Plemeniana**, **Kakodiki**, **Sarakina** and **Vlithia** and eventually reach Palaiochora, one of the towns on the south coast of Crete, facing out to the Libyan Sea. In Palaiochora, we should not omit to visit **Gavdiotika**, the old part of the town, built with narrow alleys by fishermen from Gavdos, beneath a hill on which are the ruins of a Venetian castle. There is an interesting **Historical Museum** in the town, with important exhibits from the period around the War of Independence. Nearby is the **Anydri-Yaniskari gorge**, and to the west of the town is the superb beach of **Pacheia Ammos**. Little boats ply back and forth along the coast each day, linking Palaiochora with **Souyia**, **Ayia Roumeli** and **Chora Sfakion**, and sailing out three times a week to Gavdos, the most southerly inhabited place in Europe. According to the myths, Gavdos is Calypso's island of Ogygia, where Odysseus was shipwrecked. We continue in a northerly direction, coming first to the village of **Moni** and then to the upland settlement of **Rodovani** - with interesting churches - and next **Temenia**. If we carry on along this dirt track we will arrive in **Souyia**, thus avoiding the need to take the boat from Palaiochora. Souyia stands on an attractive site along a pretty beach of small pebbles and is a popular tourist resort. The modern church of the village contains a fine mosaic which originated in a sixth-century basilica. We return to Rodovani and head back to Chania along a different route which takes us through **Maralia, Kampanos**, the beautiful village of **Epanochori** with views to the White Mountains and the Libyan Sea, and **Ayia Eirini**, a tiny hamlet on the banks of a seasonal

p. 72

The Church of Christ the Saviour - a Byzantine building with important wall-paintings.

river. Beyond Ayia Eirini is a passable road through
the White Mountains to Omalos. If we take this route,
we will go through the mountain villages of **Prasies**,
Nea Roumata and **Skines** before reaching **A-
likianos**. There, among orchards, are the ruins of the
magnificent **Da Molin tower**, and there is also a
Byzantine church of St George, built in 1243 and
with fifteenth-century wall-paintings by Provatas. We
travel on through **Ayia**, where there was an open
prison for Greek patriots during the German occupation, and thence back to Chania.

4. Chania - Kolymbari - Kaloudiana - Kastelli Kissamou - Platanos - Falasarna - Chrysoskalitissa Monastery - Elafonisos; return via Elos and the Topolia gorge

This itinerary will show us something of the western
part of the Prefecture. We leave Chania in a westerly
direction and enter the subprefecture of Kissamos. We
soon come once more to **Tavronitis**, where there is
the junction for **Kantanos** and **Palaiochora**. A deviation from our route, to the west, will take us first to
the pretty village of **Kolymbari**, at the head of the
Bay of Chania, and then a little further north, to **Gonia Monastery**, in the west corner of Kydonia Bay.
The Monastery (dedicated to Our Lady Hodeghetria)
was founded in 1618 and has a good collection of old
manuscripts, codices, post-Byzantine icons and ecclesiastical vessels. To the north of the monastery stands
the building of the **Orthodox Academy of Crete**, a
modern ecclesiastical, religious and intellectual centre. Nearby is the **monument to the Greek officer
cadets** who fell in the Battle of Crete. After 25 km.
from Chania we deviate from our main route once
more (right), to visit the village of **Rodopou** and the
east side of **Cape Spathas**, where stands the **Dik-**

tynnaion, a sanctuary of the second century BC dedicated to Artemis Diktynna, on the ruins of a still earlier sacred building. We return to the main route and pass through **Kaloudiana** before coming to **Kastelli Kissamou** (42 km.). This is a small town which serves as the 'capital' of the subprefecture of Kissamos. It is fringed by a superb sandy beach. The town took its name from its 'kastello', a Venetian fortress. Seven kilometres to the south are the ruins of ancient **Polyrrhenia**. We head west from Kastelli for **Falasarna**, passing through **Platanos**, where much garden produce is grown, and turning to the right there into the plain of Falasarna. The beach where the cultivated land ends is one of the best in Crete, with fine sand and pretty coves. Here we can visit the ruins of **ancient Phalasarna**, where there are traces of a temple of Artemis (or Apollo) and the foundations of houses. In antiquity, this city - which took its name from one of the nymphs - was a centre for trade. According to our sources, it had a safe, enclosed harbour linked to the sea by a channel. Today, the water has receded and the site is dry and suitable for cultivation.

We return to **Platanos** and continue our itinerary with visits to the seaside fishing village of **Sfinari**, to **Kambos** (at an altitude of 340 m.), to **Keramoti** and to **Kefali**, where a number of roads meet. From there, we can continue in a southerly direction to **Vathi**, and then along a very poor road to the **Chrysoskalitissa Monastery**. The fortress-like foundation stands on top of a steep rock with a superb view out over the Libyan Sea. It takes its name from a golden staircase ('chrysi skala') which, according to tradition, the sinful are unable to see.

A poor road takes us on beyond the monastery to **Elafonisi**, a little island linked to the mainland by a shallow ford 800 metres long. Here the landscape is truly magical, with the calm sea all about. We can vis-

p. 75

Above: Part of the fortification towers of the harbour of ancient Phalasarna.

Below: The steep and craggy hill on which ancient Phalasarna stood.

◄ p. 76 -77

At the top western side of cape Vouxa are two islets : Agria(wild) Gramvousa and IMERI (Tame) Gramvousa. They are inaccessible and were one of oldest lairs of the Mediterranean Pirates.

it the marble plaque on the top of the island which commemorates the slaughter of 40 men and 600 women and children by Ibrahim at Easter 1824. However, access to Elafonisos is much easier by boat from Palaiochora. We return to Kefali; from here, we can move north to visit **Elos** (where chestnuts are grown) and **Strovles** (from which the road goes on to Kantanos). We continue along the main road, climbing, and after a total of 50 km. come to the village of **Kartsomado**, through which passes the **Topolia gorge** with its plane trees and wild olives. The gorge has high, sheer sides, in which there are numerous cavities like shallow caves. One of these is the **Ayia Sofia cave**, one of the finest caverns on Crete, with superbly-shaped stalactites and stalagmites. On emerging from the gorge we come to the village of **Topolia**, a pretty settlement built on a naturally amphitheatrical site in a hilly area where there are many streams. The village is traditional in character, with tiled houses and numerous little squares. In and near the village are Byzantine churches, such as the **twin-aisled church of St Paraskeve**, the **church of St George** at **Tsourouniana**, and the **church of St Panteleimon** at **Aligiziana**. Our route back to Chania takes us first to Kaloudiana and then along the main Kissamos - Chania road.

5. Chania - Omalos plateau - Samaria Gorge - Ayia Roumeli - Chora Sfakion - Frangokastello - Vryses

p. 79 ►

The Samaria Gorge. View of the 'Portes', where the Gorge narrows to 3 - 4 metres. The sheer walls rise to a height of 500 metres.

We head south from Chania along the most popular itinerary in Crete, one which involves a walk of 6-8 hours down the most beautiful gorge anywhere in Europe. The itinerary can be covered in a single day. However, note that private transport is not convenient for those wishing to walk down the gorge; it is in any

p. 80

A: Xyloskalo. The highest point and entrance of the Samaria Gorge.

B: A point on the enchanting route through the Gorge.

C: The ravine at the point where it narrows and towering rocks on either side almost meet.

case hard to walk back up again, and the return trip certainly cannot be done in a single day. We head out of Chania along the Omalos road, in a southerly direction. We first pass through the **Keritis valley**. From **Fourne**, a pretty village set about with orange groves in the Keritis valley, the road climbs into the White Mountains. The route between here and **Xyloskalo**, where we enter the Samaria Gorge, is one of the greatest beauty. The only village along the way is **Lakki**, a historic place whose position high in the mountains helped it play an important part in the Cretan struggle for freedom. The part of the road from Lakki to the highest point on the route - from which the **Omalos**

plateau is visible - is the **Mousouri road**, known to all Greeks from songs about the freedom-fighters of Crete. At the entrance to the plateau are the house and tomb of Hadzimichalis Yannaris, one of the leaders of the struggle for liberty. The road passes along the west side of the plateau and ends at **Xyloskalo**, a position of strategic importance throughout all the fighting in Crete. Nowadays, the steps down into the gorge are cut out of the rock and the descent is easy. Once, however, a staircase made of treetrunks served both those descending and those ascending, and gave its name to the whole area ('Xyloskala' = 'wooden staircase'). At the top of the gorge is a small hostel with a superb

p. 81

A: The Chapel of St Nicholas.

B: Ayia Roumeli.

C: The new village of Ayia Roumeli consists of two settlements and a fine beach.

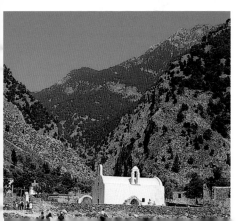

view. Shortly before Xyloskalo, a minor road leads up
to the ski centre at Kallergi, where the altitude is 1680
metres. The footpath into the gorge starts at Xyloskalo. The Samaria Gorge is the longest in Europe: 18 k-
ilometres, of which visitors walk 14. It has been scheduled as a national park so as to preserve the flora, fauna and avifauna which live in the area, and the Cretan
wild goat in particular. It is only permitted to walk
through the Gorge from early May to late October: in
the winter months, the water in the stream-bed flows
rapidly, and landslides across the path are not un-
known. As we walk through the gorge we pass the
chapel of St Nicholas, where there are tall cypress
trees and cool springs. Nearby was the site of the
Doric city of Caino. Here we are at the bottom of the
gorge, with mountains rising to 2,000 metres on either
side of us. After this point the walking becomes easier, and smaller ravines open out to the left and right of
the 'Faranga', as the Samaria Gorge is locally known.
Halfway along is the old village of Samaria; now it is
uninhabited, as the few families of woodcutters who
used to live there moved out when the area was made
a national park. There is a **Byzantine chapel** of the
fourteenth century dedicated to the **Blessed Mary of
Egypt** - whose Greek name ('Osia Maria') was gradually corrupted into 'Sia Maria' and thus 'Samaria', coming to denote the entire area. This is a good place to
stop and snack on what we have brought with us. We
now come to **Portes** ('doors'), so called because at this
point the walls of the gorge come so close together as
to give the impression that there is no way forward at
all. Little by little, however, the gorge widens out,
reaching the abandoned upper village of Ayia
Roumeli. A little way further on is the new village of
Ayia Roumeli, in an isolated spot by the sea some 1.5
km. from the mouth of the gorge. There is no way to
reach Ayia Roumeli by road from the rest of the Pre-

p. 83

*Above: The attra-
ctive seaside village
of Loutro, on the site
of the ancient town
of Phoenix.*

*Below: Very close to
Loutro stands a
small chapel built
before the 15th
century and
dedicated to St Paul.*

fecture. The only way to enter or leave (apart from the gorge) is by launch to the west, to Souyia and Palaiochora (buses to Chania), or to the east, to Loutro and Chora Sfakion. Loutro stands behind a little beach among the arms of the mountain as they sweep down to the sea. **Sfakia** (or **Chora Sfakion**) is a historic village in a rocky and arid region which is difficult to approach either by land or by sea. Its name comes from the word *sphax,* meaning a chasm in the ground: this, then, is the land of ravines. As a result of its position, it was never fully under Turkish control and many of the Cretan revolts centred on it. It has been the scene of fierce fighting throughout its history. We can now return directly to Chania. Alternatively, we could visit the village of **Anopoli**, up in the mountains, the **Venetian castle** of **Frangokastello** (with a square ground plan and towers at each corner), and the village of **Vryses** on the banks of the Vrysianos river.

p. 84

Chora Sfakion. Its inaccessible position meant that it was able to resist subjugation and serve as a base for uprisings and battles.

p. 85

Above: The imposing Aradaina Gorge, between the plateaus of Anopoli and Aradaina.

Below: The Venetian Frankocastello fortress, which has survived in excellent condition.

From Vryses, the old main road from Chania to Rethymno will take us back to our starting-point.

6. Chania - Cape Kydonias - Profitis Ilias hill - Holy Trinity Monastery - Gouverneto Monastery - Lake Kourna - Rethymno

This itinerary will take us our to **Cape Kydonias** to the east of Chania. Here, at a distance of 15 km. from Chania town, is the airport. We set off from Chania in the direction of the airport, and after 4.5 km. come to a road which climbs away to the east, up **Profitis Ilias hill**. Here the revolutionaries calling for the union of Crete with Greece rallied for the first time in 1897, and here the Greek flag was raised in February 1913 to mark the achievement of their aspirations. The **tombs of Eleftherios and Sofoklis Venizelos** are located here. Further to the east, we come to **Korakies** and **Aroni**, quaint villages with houses in the traditional style. Not far beyond Aroni a side-road to the north leads to the **Monastery of the Holy Trinity 'ton Tsangarolon'**, which has a library and a collection of icons and houses the Theological Seminary of Crete. The monastery can also be reached from Profitis Ilias Hill. Four kilometres of narrow road beyond the Holy Trinity Monastery bring us to the interesting and historic **Gouverneto Monastery**, or **Our Lady of the Angels**, dedicated to the Presentation of Our Lady. The monastery is at an altitude of 280 metres and was built in 1548; the fact that this was during the Venetian period can be seen from the Renaissance sculptures on the facade. On the west side of the monastery is the narthex, with chapels dedicated to St John the Hermit and the Ten Holy Martyrs. Nearby is the cave known as **Arkouditissa** or **Arkoudia**, where the goddess Artemis was worshipped in antiquity. Also close at hand, to the north of the Gouverneto Monastery, are the ruins of the **Monastery of St John the Hermit** or

'**Xenou**', locally known as '**katholiko**'. This is believed to have been the first Christian church built in
Crete, in the sixth or seventh century. On the west
coast of the cape we can visit the seaside village of
Kalathaki, which has a good beach and tourist a-
menities. We return to the Holy Trinity Monastery and
bear left for the airport, thus completing our circuit of
Cape Kydonias.

Now we return to Chania and take the elm-lined
road that leads to **Souda**, 6 km. away, the huge natural harbour at the head of the bay by the same name.
Souda is the main gateway to the sea not only for Chania but for the whole of Crete. It takes its name from
the Latin word suda, meaning a narrow channel.

Off the main road to Rethymno, we can visit the village of **Malaxa**, in a panoramic position at an altitude
of 500 m. There is a fine gorge and a cave. Nearby is
ancient Aptera: the name of the city ('wingless ones')

p. 87

*Panoramic aerial
photograph of the
Monastery of the
Holy Trinity of the
Tsangaroli. The
Monastery was built
in the seventeeth
century.*

is attributed by the myths to the Sirens, who, having been defeated in a musical contest by the Muses, plucked off their wings and feathers in grief and, pale and bare, plunged into the sea where they formed the islets called **Lefkes** in the mouth of Souda Bay. There are ruins of an early first-century BC temple where Demeter and Kore were probably the deities worshipped. Huge Roman cisterns and imposing 'Cyclopean' walls have survived in good condition, and there are traces of a theatre. If we continue along the main road, we will pass through **Megala Chorafia** and the little village of **Kalami** before reaching a possible stopping point in the seaside settlement of **Kalyves**. We can visit the ruins of the **Venetian fortress of Apicorno**, which gave its name to the subprefecture of Apokoronou. We carry on through **Almyrida**, **Gavalochori** (with numerous churches and chapels) and **Vamos**, chief town of the subprefecture of Apokoronou. The town is the most important administrative and commercial centre in the vicinity, and took its name from the Arabic word 'vamos', meaning passage or crossing.

Now we come to **Yeorgioupoli**, a coastal town behind which is the Armyros plain. Its position by the sea gave the town its old name of Armyros ('salty') or Armyroupoli, but it was later named Yeorgioupoli in honour of Prince George, High Commissioner of Crete. All the bustle of the tourist trade centres on the square with its towering eucalyptus trees, the seafront and the little harbour where the Almyros river runs into the sea. Among the nearby sights is **Lake Kourna**, the only lake on Crete, set in a landscape which is very relaxing on the eye. A cave by the same name is to the south of the lake. We can climb up to the village of **Kourna**, on the slopes of Mt Dafnomadara. We return to the main road; through Yeorgioupoli we can drive on to **Vryses**, and from there turn south for Chora Sfakion or continue our trip into the Prefecture of Rethymno.

◀ *p. 88*

View of the seaside town of Georgioupoli, which has developed into a popular tourist resort.

p. 90-91 ▶

Kournas Lake, the only lake in Crete, has an area of 6.5 hectares and a depth of up to 25 metres.

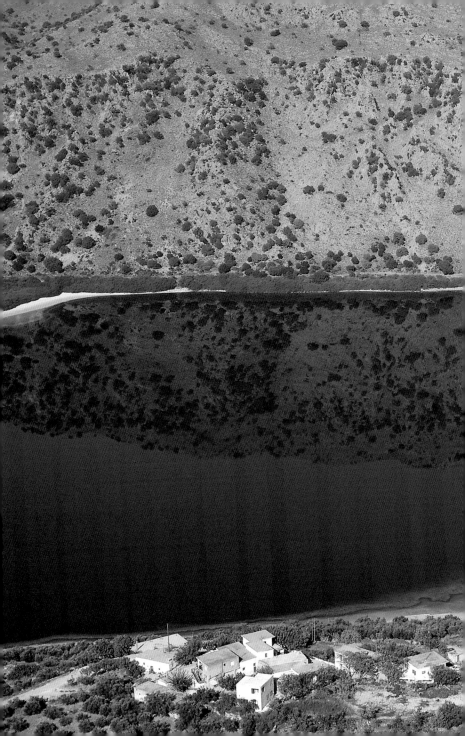

2. The Prefecture of Rethymno

The Prefecture of Rethymno is located in the centre of Crete, to the east of the Prefecture of Chania. It has an area of 1,496 square kilometres, its capital is Rethymno, and it is divided into four subprefectures: those of Mylopotamos, Ayios Vasileios, Amari and Rethymno itself. This is the most mountainous of the prefectures of Crete, but at the same time it has the best beaches in western Crete, with abundant resorts and large-scale tourist units. With the exception of the Idaean Cave, where the myths place the birth of Zeus, of ancient Eleftherna and of Axos, the Prefecture has little to show in the way of archaeological sites.

RETHYMNO

p. 93 ▶

View of part of the harbour. The fortress of Fortezza can be seen in the background, on the Palaiokastro hill. In front can be seen the large Turkish lighthouse on the northern 'arm' of the harbour.

Rethymno, capital of the Prefecture by the same name and the administrative and commercial centre for the surrounding area, is the smallest of the historic cities of Crete. This picturesque town has been untouched by earthquakes and has retained its blend of Eastern mystique and Western grandeur. There are numerous Venetian houses and churches; the latter were converted into mosques during the period of Turkish rule. Clustered around its Fortezza (fortress), Rethymno will make an immediate and lasting impression on visitors, to which its disused minaret will undoubtedly contribute.

History

Human habitation of the site occupied by Rethymno dates back to Late Minoan or Postpalatial times, as demonstrated by the finding in 1947 of a Late Minoan burial in the suburb of Mastaba to the south of the town. The autonomous and independent city of Rithymna later grew up on the same site in the fourth and third centuries BC. This city fell into decline as early as the third century BC, and by the end of the Roman period it was no more than a large village - a status which it retained through the second period of Byzantine rule. Rethymno began to develop into a sizeable town once more under the Venetians, after

p. 94-95

General view of the harbour and town of Rethymno, showing its picturesque minarets, which give it a Levantine air.

1210, when its little harbour of Mandraki was laid out for the needs of the transit trade. Rettimo, as the town was known at that time, was the seat of the Venetian governor of the province. After the occupation of the town by the Turks in 1646, Rethymno disappeared altogether from the pages of history - despite the fact that it was the centre of administration in western Crete and the largest commercial port in the area. The people of Rethymno took part in all the revolutionary action to liberate the island and unite it with Greece.

Tour of the town

Rethymno consists of two parts, the old and the new, the latter being an extension of the former

p. 96-97

Houses in traditional style near the harbour. On street level they house tavernas and cafés.

towards the south. Since 1970, the town has also spread along the coast to the east, in the direction of the village of **Perivolia**. The town is carefully laid-out, with multistorey buildings and an adequate number of parks, but the seafront is largely hidden by large hotels. The old town, however, has plenty of surprises for the visitor: Byzantine and Venetian churches side-by-side with minarets, arched passageways, Venetian mansions, Turkish fountains, narrow alleyways and old houses with heavy wooden doors and windows. Also in the old town is the little Venetian harbour with its tall houses, vaulted shops and Turkish cannon mounted here and there.

As we walk through the old town, we will see - among other buildings - the **Loggia**, built in the sixteenth century. This is a fine, square Venetian structure, which was originally used as a meeting and recreation place for the local nobles and aristocrats. Now it houses the **Archaeological Museum**. The **Fortezza**, Rethymno's fortress, stands on Palaiokastro hill to the north of the town. It was built in 1573 by Venetian commander Alviso Lando. Today only the walls have survived (restored), together with cisterns and a mosque with a huge dome: this was originally the **cathedral of St Nicholas**, which the Turks converted into a mosque. The **Rimondi Fountain**, on the north side of Petychaki Square,

p. 98

Traditional-style bakery, with tempting Cretan confectionery in the window.

was erected in 1629 on the site of an earlier fountain by Rimondi, governor of Rethymno.

Among other interesting buildings is the **Bish-
opric**, a neo-Classical structure with an absolutely
symmetrical facade. The **Prefecture Building** is also in the neo-Classical style; built in 1869, it has a
large number of windows on two storeys. A **Turkish school** has survived next to the church of St
Francis, built in 1796 as a girls' school, as has the
Turkish baths, at 25 Radamanthous St. The **church
of St Francis**, a single-aisled wooden-roofed basilica which was used as a poorhouse in Turkish
times, was restored in 1971 and impresses the visitor with its architecture and sculptural ornamentation. The **Church of Our Lady of the Angels** dates

p. 99

*The Rimondi
Fountain, of
interest for its
architecture and
sculpture, on the
north side of
Petychaki Square.*

from the closing period of Venetian rule. It is also known as 'Our Lady the Lesser', and is located in the old town. Our Lady of the Angels is a three-aisled church without a dome, dedicated to St Mary Magdalene by the Dominican order of monks. The **Cathedral of the Presentation of the Virgin**, a new church modelled on the Church of the Annunciation on Tinos, has a fine carved wooden screen and good modern wall-paintings. It also preserves an outstanding portable Byzantine icon of Our Lady of Passion, unsigned and undated.

Museums

The **Archaeological Museum**, housed in the Loggia (on the corner of Katechaki and Himara Sts), has a collection of exhibits covering the period from the

p. 100

The city still has its old shops where traditional crafts are still practised, such as the coppersmith's in the picture, with its cauldrons.

Neolithic era to Turkish times (tel. nos. 29975, 20668). The **L. Kanakakis Art Gallery and Centre for Contemporary Art** has work by the painter Lefteris Kanakakis and a collection of 45 paintings by other Greek artists dating from the period after 1950 (corner of Himara and Ioannou Melissinou Sts, tel. no. 21847). The **Historical and Folklore Museum of Rethymno** was founded in 1974 by the Historical and Folklore Association of Rethymno and has a collection of historical and folklore exhibits, woven goods and paintings (tel. no. 23667). The **Folklore Collection of the Lyceum of Greek Women** is housed in a building belonging to the Lyceum at 18 Mesolongiou St. The collection was founded in 1963 and consists of embroidery, woven goods, wood-carvings, local costumes, pottery and utensils (tel. no. 29572).

p. 101

Fish shop in the old style, with a variety of fresh-caught fish.

Trips starting from Rethymno

Shorter routes

1. Rethymno - Arkadi Monastery

Among the important sites near Rethymno is the **Arkadi Monastery**, a sacred symbol of liberty. It stands 22 km. along the road from Rethymno to Herakleio, on the edge of a fertile plateau, with a view to the hills behind and down to the sea. The inaccessibility of the site on which the monastery stands combined with the manner of its construction - with high, thick walls - to determine its history. The Monastery consists of a fortified block with two main entries, guesthouses, a refectory, cellars and a gunpowder store. It may have been founded in the second period of Byzantine rule (by a monk called Arkadios), or perhaps in the sixteenth century, if we are to believe the inscription on the bell-tower. The main church is a two-aisled basilica dedicated to St Constantine and the Transfiguration of Our Lord. On 7-9 November each year, there are celebrations to mark the anniversary of the holocaust of the Monastery, in 1866, when its defenders blew up the gunpowder store - and themselves - so as not to fall into the hands of the Turks. In the museum of the Monastery is a collection of mementoes, including the bones of the freedom fighters killed when the Monastery exploded.

p. 103 ➤

The historic Arkadi Monastery (fourteenth century). Its most important and best preserved feature is its church, with its facade in the Renaissance style.

2. Rethymno - Asi Gonia - Myriokefala

From Rethymno, we take the old main ('national') road towards Chania, coming to the village of **Atsitopoulo** and then to **Prines**, with an interesting **church of St Nicholas**. After 16 km. along this road we can turn left to visit the village of **Ayios Konstantinos**, with attractive villas and mansions which must have been the summer residences of the Venetian overlords of Rethymno. In **Roustika**, nearby, is the **Monastery of the Prophet Elijah**. We continue along the main road, travelling through the fertile valley of the river Mouselas to **Megali Episkopi**, the last village in the Prefecture of Rethymno in a westerly direction. From this point we can visit **Argyroupoli**, a village which stands on a charming site at an altitude of 260 m. between the Mouselas and Petre rivers.

Here the road divides. If we bear right, we will reach the pretty village of **Asi Gonia**, in the sub-prefecture of Apokoronou. The village stands at an altitude of 480 m. and will provide a relaxing note with its plentiful streams and abundant shade. Since Venetian times, Asi Gonia has been the natural frontier between the Rethymno and Chania areas. In fact, it is now administratively part of the Prefecture of Chania, but access to it is easier from the Rethymno side. Its natural position - easy to fortify and difficult to approach - made it a centre for Cretan revolutionaries, as its name, meaning 'Rebels' Corner', impies (the Arabic word 'asi' means 'brave fellow' and, by extension, 'rebel'). Turning left in Argyroupoli will bring us to the mountain village of **Myriokefala**, whose name comes from the 'myria' ('many') 'kefala' ('heads', or 'hills') in the vicinity. The area is well-known for the **Myriokefalon Monastery**, built at an altitude of 500 m., which has its feast day on 8 September.

Longer routes

3. Rethymno - Kourtaliotiko Gorge - Preveli Monastery - Damioni - Plakias - Myrthios - Rodakino - Kotsyfou Gorge

We complete our tour of the western part of the Prefecture of Rethymno by leaving the town in a southerly direction, towards the hinterland. After driving through olive groves and oak forests we reach **Armeni**, at an altitude of 380 m. In the vicinity, 167 shaft tombs hewn out of the rock have been found. After 19 km. we come to a turning on our right, which leads to the village of **Ayios Vasileios** and the Kotsyfou Gorge. The road straight ahead leads through the wonderful **Kourtaliotiko Gorge**, by which the Kourtaliotikos River passes between Mt Kouroupa and Mt Xiro Oros. As we emerge from the gorge, shortly before the village of **Asomatos**, a road to the left

p. 105

Preveli Monastery, built (probably around 1701) on a rocky site with an enchanting view over the Libyan Sea.

leads through a verdant landscape to **Preveli Monastery**, which stands high on a bare rock looking out to sea. The Monastery, dedicated to St John the Divine, was founded in the sixteenth or seventeenth century. Like almost all the monasteries in Crete, it had an important part to play in the island's struggle for freedom. In the Monastery is a gold crucifix studded with pieces of the True Cross and precious stones which is believed to be wonderworking. A footpath sets out across the rocks from the Monastery and leads us to one of the most idyllic natural settings in south Crete, **Preveli beach**, where the Kourtaliotikos river runs into the sea. We return to Asomatos and continue our itinerary, heading left. Along this route we will come to **Myrthios**, a village on a naturally amphitheatrical site with a view towards the Libyan Sea, and **Plakias**, which has developed into a popular tourist resort. From here, short trips can be made by caique to **Frangokastello**, **Preveli Monastery** and **Ayia Galini**. To the north-east of Myrthios is the **Kotsyfou Gorge**, between Mt Kouroupa and Mt Kryoneritis. At the end of the gorge the road passes through the mountain villages of **Ayios Ioannis** and **Ayios Vasileios**, the latter of which gave its name to the entire subprefecture, and then join the road back to Rethymno.

p. 106-107
The beautiful Kourtaliotis Gorge. It starts out from the village of Koxare and follows the course of the Kourtaliotis river.

4. Rethymno - Vrysinas - Amari valley - Ayia Galini - Spili

p. 108

A: The Kourtaliotis Gorge, through which the Kortaliotis river flows.

B: The seaside village of Plakias.

For this route, we head out of Rethymno in the direction of Herakleio. When we reach the village of **Perivolia**, we bear right for Amari. The main road winds up into the mountains, through **Prases** (a charming village with many Venetian houses), **Potami** with its fertile fields, **Apostoli** and **Ayia Foteini**. From here, a turning to the left will take us to

Thronos on the hill called **Throniani Kefala**, which has a superb view of Mt Psiloritis. If we go s-traight on at Ayia Foteini, we will come to the **Asomaton Monastery**, which since 1927 has functioned as a School of Farming, and to **Amari**, a little upland village which is the 'capital' of the Amari subprefecture. In order to continue along our route, we return to the main road at the Asomaton Monastery and head south, in the direction of the pretty port of **Ayia Galini** on the safe Bay of Messara, looking out to the

p. 109

Ayia Galini attracts large numbers of visitors each year with its plentiful tourist accommodation and facilities, together with the natural beauty of the landscape and its fine beaches.

Libyan Sea. In the space of just a few years, Ayia Galini has changed from being a simple fishing village into a bustling resort. Along the coast to the west of the village are caves which can be visited only by boat. Near Ayia Galini we can visit **Tymbaki**, in the midst of a fertile farming area, the settlement of **Kokkinos Pyrgos** ('red tower': there is a medieval structure which answers this description), and **Kalyviani Monastery**. To return to Rethymno, we take the road through **Spili**, chief town of the Ayios Vasileios subprefecture. This very attractive village stands on an outcrop on the south-western slopes of Mt Kedros. The setting is verdant, with numerous streams, and the courtyards of the houses are full of flowers. The little square with its 25 fountains, where cool water pours from sculpted lions' heads, will revive and relax us shortly before the return route ends and we reach Rethymno.

5. Rethymno - Perama - Anoyeia - the Idaean Cave - the Melidoni Cave

Now we must take the old main road in the direction of Herakleio. First we come to **Perama**, chief town of the subprefecture of Mylopotamos. Here we can turn south to visit **Margarites**, the village where the famous storage jars are made in the ancient style, and **Eleftherna**, which occupies the site of an ancient city. Ancient Eleftherna is approximately 30 km. to the south-east of Rethymno, in the foothills of Mt Psiloritis (Ida), at an altitude of approximately 380 metres above sea-level. The inhab-

p. 110

A lion's head spouts clear cooling water from a mountain spring in the village of Spili.

p. 111

*Above: In the small
village square of
Spili, 25 spouts in
the shape of lions'
heads invite the
visitor to pause for
refreshment.*

*Below: The
luxuriant green of
the village of Spili,
from a distance.*

ited area was widespread, focusing on two nuclei on natural outcrops: Prine Hill and the flat hilltop on which the modern village now stands. We can continue from here in an easterly direction; after **Mourtziana** we will come to the village of **Garazo**, in a verdant valley through which flows the river Oaxos or Yeropotamos. The same river also passes through the village of Axos, which stands below an ancient city called Axos or Oaxos. Some of the inhabitants of Axos were compelled by Venetian persecution to flee further to the east, where they founded the village of **Axika Anoyeia** or **Xinganoyeia**; this takes its name from the word 'ano', 'up', in reference to the altitude of the village, high on the northern slopes of Mt Ida just below the peak known as Armi. Anoyeia is one of the most important centres for handicrafts and cottage industries in Crete, and it is also the starting-point for the ascent of Mt Ida (Psiloritis), with access to the Idaean Cave. At **Zominthos** are traces of a Minoan villa discovered during recent excavations; further along, up a steep path, is the **Idaean Cave**. The cave is located on the superb **Nida Plateau** on Psiloritis, at an altitude of 1,538 metres; the local shepherds call it the 'Shepherd Girl's Cave'. The cavern became a place of worship in Neolithic times, and retained this function in the Minoan era. In the Hellenistic and Roman periods it retained much of its glory, but with the coming of Christianity it ceased to have any religious importance and became a shelter for shepherds. According to the myths, Rhea gave birth to Zeus in the Diktaean Cave and then brought him here to hide him from his father Kronos, who would have swallowed him. After returning to Anoyeia, we can either head west back to Rethymno or east for Herakleio.

p. 113 ►

Stockbreeding plays a very important role in the economy of Crete, as a result of its mainly mountainous terrain.

3. The Prefecture of Herakleio

The Prefecture of Herakleio is located in the centre of the island and consists of seven subprefectures: those of Temenos, Vianno, Malevizi, Pyrgiotissa, Kainourgio, Pediada and Monofatsi. The capital of the Prefecture - and of the Temenos subprefecture - is Herakleio. With a population of more than 250,000, the Prefecture of Herakleio is the most densely-inhabited part of the island, and, given that it can boast most of the important centres of Minoan civilisation (Knossos, Phaistos, Malia, Gortys, Tylissos) and the best tourist beaches, is the area most popular with visitors. The Prefecture of Herakleio is a place of great contrasts. There are extensive plains (that of Messara is the largest), tall mountains (sometimes bare and sometimes covered with cypress and oak forests), lower hills with orchards of fruit trees, long sandy beaches, and beautiful sheltered coves.

HERAKLEIO

Herakleio has developed into a modern city and into the commercial, industrial and agricultural centre of eastern Crete, handling a wealth of excellent products which include sultanas and various kinds of table grapes, such as the *razakí* variety from Archanes. The city is the capital of the Prefecture of Herakleio and, since 1972, of the whole of Crete. It is also the ecclesiastical 'capital' of the island. Herakleio has long been a cultural centre for Crete and has produced important figures in painting and literature, such as the famous Domenico Theotokopoulos ('El Greco'), the great novelist Nikos

p. 115 ▶

Part of the Venetian harbour and modern city of Irakleio.

Kazantzakis, and the historian Yannis Mourellos.

Herakleio has grown rapidly and now has a population of 125,000, making it the island's largest city. However, the fact that building has been largely unplanned and chaotic has meant that it faces the problems of the large modern city: traffic problems, and a lack of parks and open spaces. The city as such is not, then, of any great interest, with the exception, of course, of its Archaeological Museum with its wonderful collections of antiquities which have been dug from the soil of Crete. The most famous of the Minoan sites await our exploration close to the city.

History

The history of Herakleio is reflected in the way in which its name has changed through the ages. Ac-

cording to Strabo, it stands on the site of what was in
antiquity one of the ports of Knossos, known as Her-
akleia. The settlement retained this name in Roman
times. Later, in the Byzantine period, it was known as
'Castro', a reference to some fortress or fortification on
the site. But the city's real history starts in 824 AD,
when the city was taken by the Arabs. It was they who
fortified the old settlement of Herakleia-Castro and
dug a moat round it. It was from this moat - 'handax'
in Arabic - that it took the name which it kept until the
19th century. Handak served as a base for the pirate
raids of the Arabs, but it was under Venetian rule
(1204 - 1669) that it reached the peak of its prosperity: now known as Candia, it became the most important political, military, commercial and social centre of
the entire island. During this period it was fortified by

p. 116-117

*View of the harbour
with the Venetian
Koules fortress.*

its overlords with new, strong walls, the so-called Venetian walls, and adorned with handsome buildings, squares, churches, monuments and fountains. The was also the period when literature and the arts flourished in Herakleio, partly because of influences coming from Renaissance Italy and partly because on the Fall of Constantinople in 1453, many men of letters and artists took refuge in Crete. The city was surrendered to the Turks, after a 21-year siege, in 1669, when its name changed to 'Megalo Kastro' ('Great Fortress'). The presence of the Turks gave the city an Oriental appearance. The conquerors repaired the buildings which had been damaged, built new ones, converted the churches into mosques, and made good the walls. During these dark days of slavery, the city lost its former prosperity. In 1828 and 1898 there were major massacres of its population, but in 1913, together with the rest of Crete, it was finally incorporated into the Greek state.

Tour of the city

_p. 119_ ▶

Above: The Venetian Bembo Fountain (1588) stands in Kornarou Square. It has relief coats-of-arms and a headless Roman statue.

Below: The Venetian Morosini Fountain (1628), in the middle of Venizelos Square. It consists of eight basins, the highest of which rests on four lions.

Although Herakleio has been destroyed and then rebuilt many times in the course of its history, it still has a good number of monuments and sights which are worth seeing. It consists of the Old Town, enclosed by the Venetian walls, and the New Town which has spread outside these. The walls form a triangle which has the sea as its base and the **Martinengo Bastion** as its apex. A tour of the city can take as its starting-point the **Venetian harbour**, which is to the left of the large modern harbour. It was of great commercial importance under the Venetians and a major naval base. Of interest here is the **Kastro**, known as the **Koules fortress**, at the entrance to the Venetian harbour. This was built by the Venetians to protect the harbour from enemy attack. On its three sides parts of the reliefs of the lion of St Mark built into the walls have survived.

Its interior was used for warehouses, a prison, and accommodation for the guards. The fortress is open to the public, while there is an open-air theatre on top of it. The Venetian walls are the most important monuments dating from this part of the city's history. They were first built in the 15th century, with additions and improvements in the 16th and 17th. Their principle designer was one of the most distinguished military engineers of the 16th century, Michele Sammicheli from Verona. The total length of the triangular walls is three kilometres and they were protected by seven bastions, all of which have survived. Of its four gates, three can still be seen. The **Chania Gate** on the western side of the walls dates from 1570. On its inner facade a medallion containing a relief bust of Christ as the Ruler of All with the inscription *'Omnipotens'* ('Almighty') has been preserved. It is this which has given it its alternative name of the Gate of the 'Pantokrator' ('Almighty'). On the outer facade there is the winged lion of St Mark in relief and above this another relief bust of the Pantokrator, with an inscription in Greek This was the gate from which the whole of western Crete was reached. The other surviving gate is on the south side, the **Jesus Gate** or **New Gate**, dating from 1587. On its inner facade it has architectural decoration consisting of an entablature, triglyphs and metopes. In the middle can

p. 122

Street vendor of 'kouloúria' bread rings in Irakleio.

be seen an inscription giving the date of its construction and the name of the Governor of the day, Mocenigo. As the wall continues to the south, we come to the **Martinengo Bastion**. Here, on a platform, is the **tomb of Nikos Kazantzakis**, with its simple inscription: "I hope for nothing, I fear nothing, I am free". About midway along 25 Avgoustou St, which climbs from the harbour, is the square containing the **Church of St Titus**, the patron saint of Crete. Its architecture combines various Eastern and Western features, reflecting its troubled history. Here is preserved the head of St Titus, which was returned to the church in 1966 from Venice, where it was taken when Herakleio fell to the Turks. The loggia at the end of the square is the restored **Loggia of the Venetians**, which

p. 123
Part of the Venetian Loggia. This grand edifice was built c.1626-8 and served as a club for the nobility.

houses the Town Hall. This rectangular two-storey building, the centre of the public life of the nobility under Venetian rule, was built in the early 16th century. The building which stands on the site today is a faithful reproduction of the old monument. The **Basilica of St Mark** stands in Venizelou or Krinis Square, to which 25 Avgoustou St leads. It was built in 1239 by the Venetians and dedicated to their patron saint. Today it is used as the premises of the Literary Society and houses a permanent collection of copies of Byzantine wall-paintings from various churches in Crete. The **Cathedral Church of St Minas**, which is in Ayias Aikaterinis Square, was built between 1862 and 1895 and, in terms of size, is one of the island's most impressive churches. It is in the form of a cross with arms of equal length, topped with a dome. At the western corner of the Cathedral is the small, older **Church of St Minas**, with fine carved wood decoration and 18th century icons, and the old **Church of the Presentation of Christ**. Other buildings of interest include the **Vikelaian Library**, which is housed in the **'Aktarika' municipal building**, the **Public Services Building** - once the Turkish barracks and now the prefecture offices and law courts - and the picturesque **Public Market**. The city has kept fountains from the Venetian period: the **Morosini Fountain**, in the middle of Venizelou Square, the **Bembo Fountain**, in Kornarou Square, and the Priouli or **Delimarkou Fountain** in Delimarkou St, in the northern part of the city.

p. 124
Vessel in the 'marine' style, decorated with octopuses.

Museum

The **Archaeological Museum** is housed in a two-storey building in Xanthoudidi St, on the north-eastern side of Eleftherias Square (tel. nos 226092, 226470). It has 20 rooms and its exhibits come exclusively from Crete itself, covering a period from the Neolithic Age to the end of the Helleno-Roman period (4th century AD). The **Historical and Folklore Museum** (7 Kalokairinou St - tel. no. 283219) is in a building which was once the residence of a great benefactor of Crete, Andreas Kalokairinos. The continuity of Cretan culture can be traced through its collections, which are arranged chronologically and by subject-matter in the rooms of this three-storey building. The **St Catherine Collection of Byzantine Icons**, also called the **Museum of Church Art**, is to be found in the 15th century **Basilica of St Catherine**, in Ayias Aikaterinis Square. It contains artefacts used in Christian worship: icons, wood-carvings, wall-paintings, manuscripts and ecclesiastical books. Of particular interest are six icons by the Cretan icon-painter Michael Damaskinos, dating from between 1582 and 1591.

p. 125

Above: Kamares ware vessel. (Irakleio Archaeological Museum)

Below: Krater with flower decoration from the old palace at Phaistos (1800 BC). (Irakleio Archaeological Museum)

p. 126

A, B & C: Fruit stand and vessels of Kamares ware, dating from c.1800 BC. (Irakleio Archaeological Museum - Room III)

p. 127 ➤

Rhyton of rock crystal, found in the Zakro palace and dating from c.1450 BC. (Irakleio Archaeological Museum)

p. 128

A: Gold jewellery from the Tekes cemetery.

B: Figurine of a maiden with hands raised in an attitude of worship. (Irakleio Archaeological Museum)

C: Figurine of the chthonic 'Snake Goddess' in faience (c.1600 BC). (Irakleio Archaeological Museum)

p. 129 ▶

The two sides of the famous clay Phaistos Disk with a text in a hieroglyphic script which has never been deciphered. The characters are stamped on both sides and the inscription runs from the outside to the centre. It dates from 1700 - 1600 BC. (Irakleio Archaeological Museum)

Trips starting from Heracleio

Shorter routes

1. A visit to Knossos

For those without their own means of transport there is a bus service to Knossos, which is five kilometres south-west of Herakleio. Its palace, the most imposing of all the Minoan palaces, was built around 1900 BC on the Kefala hill on the site of an earlier Neolithic settlement. After the major destruction of 1700 BC, a grander building replaced this, to survive down to the the invasion of the Achaeans in c. 1450 BC. Most of what remains today dates from the brilliant Neopalatial period. Systematic excavation of the site was begun in 1900 by Sir Arthur Evans, who has not escaped criticism for the way in which he restored the palace.

We enter the **archaeological site of Knossos** from the west porch. It was from here that processions (as shown on the bases of altars which have been found here) set out. We then follow the ritual route, the Corridor of the Procession (so called from the paintings of a procession found on its walls), which led to the Stepped Portico, probably the property of some nobleman. A bridge links this with the Caravanserai, which was opposite the southern

p. 131 ➤
The northern entrance to the Palace of Knossos. The platform (bastion) has been restored and the relief painting of the bull reconstructed on it.

side of the great palace. It was in this building, which served as a place of purification or a public bath, that the famous wall-painting with the hoopoes and partridges was found. Since the processional corridor cannot be followed throughout its length, we must turn left, which brings us to the South Propylaeum, with the large double horns, the symbol of the Minoan religion. From this point the Great Staircase leads to the upper floor, the Piano Nobile, which housed the official quarters. At the top of the staircase we pass through a doorway into an antechamber and then into the central hall with its three columns. We then come to the Great Hall, the 'accounts office' of Knossos. It was from here that the clay tablets inscribed with Linear B script probably fell to the floor below. The Hall of the Frescoes contains copies of wall-paintings

p. 132

The great Southern Propylaeum. The sacred double horns can be seen in the background on the left on a special base.

found in the palace (bull-fighting scene, 'ladies in blue', saffron-gatherers, miniature wall-paintings). From the Hall of the Frescoes the Throne Room, on the north-western side of the central courtyard, is reached by a spiral staircase. The Throne Room consists of an antechamber, now containing a copy of a wooden throne, benches and a stone basin, and of the room of the throne itself. In this room, believed to have served as a religious court, is the gypsum throne of Minos, with griffins, symbolising strength, painted left and right on the walls. A staircase, next to the antechamber of the Throne Room, leads to the upper floor, where there were rooms for ritual purposes and a sanctuary. At the foot of this staircase is the palace's central sanctuary, containing two rooms with square columns in the middle, the so-called Pillar Crypts - which were

p. 133

The Southern Propylaeum has been restored in its western part, where a copy of part of the wall-painting of the 'Procession' has also been set up.

p. 135 ▶

Above: Copy of a wall-painting from the 'Room of the Frescoes'.

Below: Copy of a wall-painting on the eastern wall of the palace showing 'figure-of-eight' shields.

p. 134

The 'Queen's Megaron', with a copy of the 'Dolphins' wall-painting over the entrance.

of a sacred character - the Room of the Tall Pithos, and the Treasury. On the south-western side of the central court is a copy of the famous wall-painting 'The Prince with the Lilies'. Here, near the southern entrance, is the Sanctuary of the Double Axes. Almost in the middle of the east wing of the palace is the Grand Staircase, which divides the wing into its northern section, which contained workshops and storerooms, and the south-eastern part, which was the quarters of the royal couple.

Of particular interest are the Hall of the Double Axes and the Queen's Megaron, the wall of which, over the entrance, is decorated with a copy of the wall-painting of the dolphins. To the north-east are storerooms and the so-called Corridor of the Draught-board (from a fine draught-board which was found here), while the Queen's Bathroom, a s-

p. 137 ►

*The 'Throne Room'.
Against the northern wall
stands the stone throne of
Minos. On its right and
left griffins - symbolising
power - are painted on
the wall.*

p.136

*Above: Earthernware
basin in a small room on
the western side of the
"Queen's Megaron".*

*Below: The antechamber
to the 'Throne Room'. A
wooden throne (copy),
seats and a stone basin
can be seen.*

mall room with a bath and with a drainage system, is to the north-west. Outside the palace is the customs-house, the container for ritual purification, and the theatre. From the theatre a paved road leads to the little Palace, on the north-western side of the main palace. It is also possible to visit the Royal Villa, to the north-east of the palace and an adjunct to it, the House of the High Priest, and the Royal Tomb, one kilometre from the palace. Also of interest is the Stratigraphy Museum, with a stratigraphical collection from the excavations on the site.

2. Herakleio - Amnisos - Karteros - Cave of Eileithyia - Angarathos Monastery - Nirou Khani - Limani Chersonisou - Mochos - Stalida - Mallia

To follow this route, we leave Herakleio by the old national road to the east. We come first to the seaside village of **Nea Alikarnassos**, which is where Herakleio's international airport is sited. Crossing the fertile valley of Karteros, we reach the attractive **Karteros beach** and the ruins of **ancient Amnisos**. It was here that the Minoan 'Villa of the Frescoes' - of the Middle Minoan period, with magnificent wall-paintings (such as the famous 'lilies frescoes') - was discovered. We turn right at the Karteros junction, to reach the **Cave of Eileithyia**. This fine cave was dedicated to the goddess of childbirth and daughter of Hera, Eileithyia. This is one of the island's most ancient religious centres, in use as early as the Neolithic age as a place of worship. Its many stalactites and stalagmites were probably objects of worship. Of great interest is a rectangular altar in the centre of the cave, flanked by two cylindrical stalagmites in the form of a woman

◄ *p. 138-139*

Aerial photograph of the archaeological site of Knossos

p. 141

Above: Limin Chersonisou lies on the western edge of the Gulf of Malia.

Below: Limin Chersonisou has developed into a well-organised tourist resort.

and a man (or mother and child). A little further on is the **Angarathos Monastery**, one of the oldest in Crete, dedicated to the Dormition of the Virgin. The main road leads to the attractive beach of **Khani Kokkini**. This is close to the **archaeological site of Nirou**, where a Minoan mansion, the 'House of the High Priest' was discovered.

If we then take the new national road, we come to **Limani Chersonisou**, on the west edge of the Gulf of Mallia, a highly organised tourist resort. South of the harbour is the picturesque village of **Chersonisos**. We come next to the tourist village of **Stalida** and the pretty village of **Mochos**, before

p. 142-143
Aerial photograph
of Chersonisos.

reaching the attractive, but very busy, resort of **Mallia**. This was the city of an important Minoan city with its own palace, the name of which is not known (the name 'Mallia' comes from a Greek name which refers the levelness of the ground). The palace, which was built around 1900 BC, was destroyed for the first time in 1700 BC, was rebuilt, and then was completely destroyed in 1450 BC. Although it has the same layout as the palace of Knossos, it is less imposing because of its provincial character. It is, however, of interest for its complex design and its multiplicity of original details. Covering 8,800 sq. metres, it was of two storeys and has an oblong central courtyard, surrounded by four wings

p. 145 ▶

*Above: The arch-
aeological site of
Malia. The most
important feature
of the excavations
is the palace.*

*Below: View of
Malia's fine beach.*

p. 146-147

Chersonisos.

p. 144

*The attractive bay of
Stalida.*

and five entrances. It also has sanctuaries, worshops and storerooms. The palace is entered from a large square, paved with blue limestone and crossed with roads surfaced with stone brought from nearby quarries. Before visiting the palace, we can first go to a modern building of reinforced concrete which protects the remains of a room with columns, once underground, known as the 'Hypostyle Crypt'. In all probability this served as a building for deliberation for the authorities with many annexes. Around the palace there were various quarters which made up the Minoan city, the excavation of which has been begun by the French School of Athens.

A little further on, 500 metres north of the palace, in the **Chrysolakkos area**, a square building with grave compartments was found. There is little doubt that this was a royal cemetery, consisting of an enclosure flanked by squares on each of the four sides and perhaps by a colonnade on the east.

In the interior, the enclosure was divided into compartments by walls which formed many rooms, probably without a door, as the burials took place from above, where they were covered with large stone slabs. In the centre there was a room where a flame must have been kept burning. In the eastern wall, on the inside of the enclosure, were rooms devoted to the worship of the dead and of the Great Goddess, who is represented in many figurines.

Longer routes

3. Herakleio - Archanes - Vathipetro - Apanosifis Monastery -Viannos - Kastelli - Thrapsano - Ayies Paraskies

To follow this route, we leave Herakleio by the road to **Knossos**. Leaving Knossos on the right and the village of **Spilia**, we come to the picturesque town of **Epano Archanes**, which stands on the side of a low hill in a fertile, well-watered area. At a distance of 4.5 km. to the north is the village of **Kato Archanes**. In this village recent excavations have brought to light an exceptionally well-preserved building which must have been a palace, if we are to judge from the quality of its decoration, the size of the rooms, the wall-paintings, and the floors, which are painted or made of red and blue slate. A Minoan cemetery has been found at **Fourni**, one kilometre to the north-west of Acharnes, the largest prehistoric necropolis ever found in Crete. It consists of beehive tombs with compartments carved out of the rock and groups of shaft graves. At **Anemospilia**, 4 km. to the south-west of Archanes, is the only Minoan temple ever to be discovered. This tripartite sanctuary, built of dressed stones and surrounded by an enceinte, was the site of an altar - and the four human skeletons found here have led archaeologists to the conclusion that it was used for human sacrifice. A road to the south of Archanes brings us to the uninhabited village of **Vathypetro**, on the south-eastern slope of Mt Youchta, where, at the attractive spot known as **Piso Livadia**, the ruins of a Minoan villa were found, dating from around 1600 - 1550 BC. This was a particularly spacious building, with a central courtyard, a sanctuary room, a large hall with four square columns, and a store-room with two columns, in which storage jars and mortars were found. In the northern part of the s-toreroom a pit was discovered in which there were upturned cups sealed with plaster, which almost certainly means that offerings were made here as part of certain rituals. Of particular interest are the underground parts of the villa, where an oil-press, equipment for weaving and a wine-press were found in almost perfect condition. As we continue on our route, it is worth stopping off at the **Monastery of St George Apanosifis**, which was once an important spiritual centre for the clergy.

p. 149

Archaeological site of Archanes. Excavations have brought to light a Minoan sanctuary, beehive tombs with compartments carved out of the rock, and groups of shaft tombs.

Next we come to **Pyrgos**, the capital of the sub-prefecture of Monofatsi, where we follow the southern arterial road going eastwards. Near the village of Skinia we follow a south-easterly direction to the villages of **Epano** and **Kato Viannos**. We follow the road to **Arkalochori**, an important commercial and administrative centre. Here the Byzantine **church of the Archangel Michael** is worth a visit. At the spot known as **Profitis Ilias** there is a cave which finds have shown to have been a place of worship of a deity of war. Our route continues towards **Kasteli Pediadas**, capital of the sub-prefecture of Pediada. This is an attractive town whose name refers to the Venetian fortress which stood on the site of today's high school. We leave Kasteli in a westerly direction, but it is worth taking the turn off to the left to visit the village of Thrapsano, an im-

p. 150

Outside Bali the coast is made up of coves and sandy beaches.

portant centre for pottery-making. We reach the end
of our route with the village of **Ayies Paraskies**, on
the plain of Peza, and **Varvari**, known until recently as **Myrtia**, the birthplace of Nikos Kazantzakis,
where there is a **Kazantzakis Museum**.

4. Herakleio - Gazi - Krousonas - Arolithos - Tylissos - Sklavokambos - Gonies - Marathos - Fodele - Ayia Pelagia - Rogdia - Moni Savvathianon

We leave Herakleio by the old national road to Chania. At the village of Gazi, which stands on the banks
of the Galanos river, we can take the road to the left
to visit **Krousonas**, the main town of the sub-prefecture of Malevizi, which stands on the foothills of
the 'Koudouni' peak of Mt Psiloreitis. Continuing a-

p. 151

*Ayia Pelagia. An
attractive bay with
a good sandy beach
and large hotels.*

long the old national road, we come to **Arolithos**, a village in the traditional style, where there are various items of folk art and craft for sale, produced in the village's famous workshops. Here too we can stop for a rest at the picturesque little coffee shop. From Arolithos a branch to the left leads to **Tylissos**, which is on the site of a very important Minoan city. Remains of three of its houses of the Late Minoan Period have been found. These houses, however, are of very monumental structure for ordinary houses and have architectural features which we encounter in Minoan palaces. They have large rooms with ample doors and windows, 'basins' (for ritual purposes) and spacious storerooms. West of Tylissos, in the Sklavokambos valley, there are the remains of a palace of the Late Minoan period. We now return to Arolithos and continue on our route to the pretty village of **Marathos**. Here we turn right in a northerly direction

p. 152

The noteworthy Byzantine Church of Our Lady at Fodele (1383). Cruciform with a dome, it stands on the site of an earlier basilica.

and come to the beautiful village of **Fodele**, which nestles in a valley full of orange trees, plane trees and reed beds, through which the Pantomountrios river runs. Here we can visit the house where the great painter Domenikos Theotokopoulos ('El Greco') was born. Before returning to Herakleio, it is worth visiting the **Moni Savvathianon** monastery, near the village of **Rogdia**, south-east of Fodele.

5. Herakleio - Paliani Nunnery - Ayia Varvara - Zaros - Gortyn - Ayia Triada - Phaistos - Matala

We start out on this route by leaving Herakleio by the road which crosses the Messara plain and heads south-west towards Ayia Triada and Mires. If we make a deviation to the right, we can visit **Ayios Myronas**, the capital of the sub-prefecture of Malevizi. When we return to our main route, we reach the village of **Neo Venerato** after 20 km. Here we take the branch to the right to the **Paliani Nunnery**, one of the oldest monastic houses on the island (early Byzantine period). When we leave Neo Venerato, our next stop is **Ayia Varvara**, which has a panoramic view and owes its name to the Church of St Barbara in the middle of the village. As we enter the village, we can see, perched on a rock, the **Church of the Prophet Elijah**, which is regarded as being the geographical centre of Crete. North-west of the village, on the hill known as **'Patela tou Prinia'**, are the remains of **ancient Rizenia**. At **'Patela'** and at **'Siderospilia'**, which was where the city's cemetery was, evidence of the art and culture of an uninterrupted period of a thousand years has been discovered. The visitor who wishes to take a trip to the villages of **Apano Riza** on the southern foothills of Mt Psiloreitis should take the road branching to the right

p. 155 ►

The Odeion of Gortyn, an important building of the Roman period. On its wall it had a large carved inscription, the 'Dodecalogue of Gortyn', consisting of 12 columns.

p. 154

The Varsamonero Monastery has fourteenth and fifteenth century wall-paintings.

and pass through the fine villages of **Panassos**, **Gergeri** and **Nivrito**. Following a deviation to the west takes us along a beautiful route to the large and historic village of **Zaros**, renowned for the quality of its water, which wells up from the Votomos and Mati springs. West of Zaro is the historic **Vrontisi Monastery**, one of the most famous in Crete. Initially a dependency of the nearby Varsamonero Monastery, it became an important centre not only of monasticism, but also for culture as a centre for literature and painting. There is a tradition that the great Cretan painter Michael Damaskinos was a member of the monastic community and painted here. The two-aisled monastery church is dedicated to St Antony and the Apostle Thomas. Paintings dating from the 14th century are preserved in the chapel of St Antony. Another important monument at the Monastery is the fountain, next to the entrance, with its fine relief decoration. West of the Vrontisi Monastery is the **Varsamonero Monastery**, in the territory of the nearby village of **Vorizia**. Of this monastery, which flourished during the first three centuries of Venetian rule, only the three-aisled 'katholikon' (main church) remains today. Among its treasures were a carved wooden throne and lectern and fine wall-paintings. The next village we come to is **Kamares**, an important centre for folk art and handicrafts. To the northeast of the village is the **Kamares Cave**, where the superb pottery known as 'Kamares Ware' was found. The

next stop on our route should be the ruins of **ancient Gortyn**, between the villages of **Aghii Deka** and **Mitropoli**. Gortyn was one of the most ancient cities on the island and was its capital in Roman and early Byzantine times. There was already a settlement here in the Minoan period, but it developed into a city when the Dorians settled here. The seats of an ancient theatre and remains of an acropolis and odeum have been found. It was on the large tablets of stone built into the wall of the odeum that the laws of the city, carved one line from left to right, the next right to left and so on, alternately, in the Doric dialect were found.. This is the famous Law Code of Gortyn, dating from the late 6th century BC and a very valuable source for the study of the epigraphy and the law of the period. Close by was the agora (marketplace) with a sanctuary to Asclepius. South of Gortyn are the ruins of the **Basilica of St Titus**. The ruins of the **ancient city of Leben** are to be found on the southern foothills of the Asterousia range, on a notional striaght line from Gortyn. This city was the port of Gortyn and renowned for its sanctuary of Asclepius. The bay which is formed between two promontories, the imposing headland of Leontas on the west and Psamidomouri on the east, is called **Lentas**. This name, a corruption of the Greek for a lion, probably owes its name to the shape of the western promontory, which looks like a huge lion. As we continue on our main route, we pass through the agricultural and commercial town of **Mires**, the capital of the Kainouriou sub-prefecture, on the way to the **Our Lady 'Kalyviani' Monastery**, **Ayia Triada** and **Phaistos**.

At **Ayia Triada**, which is 3 km. west of Phaistos, are the ruins of what was either a royal villa or a small palace, built around 1600 BC on a hill and probably used originally as a summer residence for the k-

p. 157 ▶

Above: The Basilica of St Titus (sixth century AD). Relief architectural members of the church are to be found in the Historical Museum of Irakleio.

Below: Headless statue at ancient Gortyn.

ing of Phaistos and subsequently as a place of worship. In Minoan times a paved road linked Ayia Triada with Phaistos, of which some traces remain. The design of this palace was simpler than that of the other Minoan palaces, its ground plan being in the form of the letter L. This was the site of places of worship, various rooms and commercial premises with vast storage jars. Near the villa, two circular beehive tombs were found with a rich horde of grave offerings, together with other isolated rectangular tombs (it was in one of these that the famous stone sarcophagus of Ayia Triada was discovered).

p. 158

View of the archaeological site of Ayia Triada. Excavations begun here in 1902 have brought to light a Minoan palace.

Phaistos, which stands on a hill, dominating the valley of Kato Messara, is the second most important archaeological site (area: 18,000 sq. metres) in Crete

after Knossos. Phaistos was a large independent city with its own currency, ruling over the Messara plain, with two ports, Matala and Komos. According to myth, its king was Rhadamanthus, son of Zeus. It has been proved that there were two stages in the palace's development - the period of the Old or First Palace, which was destroyed by earthquake (1900 - 1700 BC), and that of the New Palace (1650 - 1400 BC). Most of what remains today dates from the second period. We enter the archaeological site from the north-west entrance with its paved courtyard and follow the processional corridor which crosses the courtyard at an angle. On the north side of the courtyard there was a theatral area, as is demonstrated by a row of seats. Nearby is the 'Propylon' of the old temple, with only

p. 159

The archaeological site of Phaistos. Most of the buildings which can be seen today belong to the second palace (the first was destroyed by an earthquake around 1700 BC).

one column and a sanctuary. To the south are the storerooms of the Old Palace, small sanctuary rooms with double axes carved on the walls and a lustral basin. South of the sanctuary and outside the palace are the foundations of a building of strange design, the Archaic temple of Rhea. In the eastern wing, opposite the theatre, is the Grand Staircase, a fine example of Minoan architecture, which leads to the Propylaea of the New Palace, forming a colonnade. East of the colonnade there was a light-shaft with three courtyards and next to it another, open-air, courtyard. On the north side of the colonnade, an imposing staircase leads to the royal apartments. On the left of a corridor is the 'Queen's Chamber' and further north the 'King's Hall', their walls covered with paintings and with a floor paved with slabs of gypsum. On the north-east is a complex of buildings belonging to the Old Palace and an integral part of its functions. It was in one of these that the famous **Phaistos Disk** was found. The Disk has an inscription in hieroglyphics, written in a spiral on both sides, and has not yet been decoded.

Our route ends at the seaside village of **Matala**, with artificial caves carved in its rocks a characteristic feature. Now an important tourist resort, its natural harbour served in antiquity as the port of Phaistos and later of Gortyn, when the latter became capital of Messara and of the whole of Crete. The buildings of the ancient town, probably including its public buildings, were at Goula, under what is now a seaside

p. 160

Large jars found in the storerooms of Phaistos. They were intended for the storing of produce and were decorated with horizontal bands in relief.

tourist resort. Recent archaeological digs have revealed large sections of houses dating from two main building phases, one of the first - second century AD and one of the fourth - fifth century AD. It is known that in the seaside area of **Kommos**, approximately 2.5 km. north of Matala, there was a Minoan town which served as a port for Phaistos. The spot where the ancient town stood is known locally as **'Tou Spanou ta Kefalia'**. The area has been extensively excavated and has provided us with an idea of the town-planning and ekistic organisation of Minoan settlements, of the materials used and of the uses of each area.

p. 162-163 ➤

Matala.

p. 161

To the south-west of the archaeological site of Phaistos a staircase leads to th great western courtyard, which is at a level six metres lower.

4. The Prefecture of Lasithi

The picture of this prefecture is made up of fertile plains, long beaches with coarse, dark or fine sand, a rugged landscape, large towns, and villages which cling to tradition. Here too there are archaeological and historical sites of particular interest. The prefecture is remarkable for its many caves and two areas which are unique: Vaï with its wood of palm trees and the Lasithi plateau with its thousands of wind-pumps.

The Prefecture of Lasithi is at the easternmost end of Crete and has an area of 1,818 sq. km. Its capital is the picturesque port of Ayios Nikolaos, and it is divided into four sub-prefectures: Mirabello, Lasithi, Ierapetra, and Siteia. Ayios Nikolaos, like Elounta, has developed into an important tourist centre with large luxury hotels.

AYIOS NIKOLAOS

Ayios Nikolaos has been the capital of the Prefecture of Lasithi since 1904. It stands on the northwestern shore of the attractive Gulf of Mirabello, Crete's largest bay. This busy, cosmopolitan town has about 8,000 inhabitants. In spite of the fact that it is modern, and from a distance there is little to distinguish it from a contemporary megalopolis, it attracts thousands of tourists every year because of the picturesqueness of its harbour, the wealth of sightseeing which the region provides and the high quality of accommodation and services with which it can supply its visitors.

p. 165 ▶

View of the harbour of Ayios Nikolaos and the Vouliagmeni lake, with which it is linked by a small canal.

In the period when they ruled the island, the Venetians built the **Mirabello** (= beautiful view) **fortress** on the highest hill in the area, close to the sea, on a site now occupied by the municipality buildings. Its purpose was to protect the harbour, which was to the north of Ayios Nikolaos and from that time on was known as 'Porto di San Nicolo', from the dedication of a nearby chapel. Under Turkish occupation the town was uninhabited and its harbour, **Mandraki**, was used for the commercial exportation of agricultural products. Towards the end of Turkish rule, a small village began to grow up round the harbour. This took the name of Ayios Nikolaos (St Nicholas) from the old single-aisled domed church which stands on the **Limenas headland**. A characteristic feature of Ayios Nikolaos is the attractive **Voulismeni** or **'Xepatomeni' lake**, which is linked to the sea by a canal. On its north-western side there is a zoo. Ac-

p. 166-167

Aerial photograph of the town of Ayios Nikolaos.

cording to mythology, the goddesses Athena and Artemis Britomartis were accustomed to bathe here. At the northern end of the harbour, on a small headland, is the **Byzantine chapel of St Nicholas**, which gave its name to the town. Two islets add to the picturesqueness of Ayios Nikolaos. The larger is that of **Ayion Panton** ('All Saints'), on which Cretan wild goats are bred, and the smaller is called **Mikro**.

Museums

The **Archaeogical Museum** (74 Palaiologou St, tel. no. 24943) contains eight rooms with finds from excavations in eastern Crete. The **Folklore Museum** (on the ground floor of the Harbourmaster's building, tel. no. 25093) has examples of folk art and craft, textiles, wood carvings, costumes and Byzantine icons. The **Koundoureios Municipal Library** contains more than 10,000 volumes (tel. no. 24071).

p. 168 - 169 ➤

Ayios Nikolaos has highly-developed tourist facilities and traffic, due mainly to the beauty of the town and harbour.

Trips starting from Ayios Nikolaos

p. 171 ▶

Wall-painting from the Church of Our Lady 'Kera' at Kritsa.

p. 170

The three-aisled Church of Our Lady 'Kera' at Kritsa, Mirabello. The southern - and oldest - part has fourteenth century wall-paintings.

Shorter routes

1. Ayios Nikolaos - Kritsa - Lato Etera

For the visitor wishing to take a short trip from Ayios Nikolaos, a visit to the picturesque, traditional village of **Kritsa** (11 km. to the south-west), which is a built in the form of an amphitheatre on the foothills of the Kastello mountain and looks out over a plain thickly planted with olive and almond trees and the Gulf of Mirabello, is the best idea. Near the village is the **Byzantine church of Our Lady 'Kera'**. This is a three-aisled rectangular church dedicated to the Dormition of the Virgin and with important wall-paintings of the fourteenth and fifteenth centuries. North of the village, at a distance of 3 km., are the ruins of the **Dorian city of Lato**. The remains of this ancient city, which was founded in the seventh century BC and was one of the

strongest cities in Crete, spread over the slopes of two acropolises, in a landscape of wild beauty. Lato presents an imposing picture composed of walls, houses and shops in a hollow in the shape of a crater.

Excavations have brought to light early buildings, including the marketplace, with a water tank in the middle, and a small sanctuary behind it, the Prytaneion (Council House) of the third century BC, and extensive ruins of public buildings, houses and walls. From Kritsa, a narrow road leads to the **Katharo plateau**, a very green area which is a favourite for summer holidays.

2. Ayios Nikolaos - Elounta - Spinalonga - Plaka - Milatos - Selinaris

This route involves an exploration of the areas which lie to the north-west of Ayios Nikolaos. We leave the town by the coast road to the north, passing the many hotels and tourist facilities. On this road we come to **Schisma**, a seaside village which attracts large numbers of tourists. Opposite we can see the long narrow **promontory of Spinalonga**, cut off from the mainland by a canal through the isthmus, dug by French sailors in the late nineteenth

p. 172-173

Elounda is 11 km. from Ayios Nikolaos and is a very popular resort, well-equipped to welcome visitors.

century and known as the Poros Isthmus. Today Spinalonga is linked to the mainland by a narrow bridge. Opposite the northern tip of the headland is the **rocky islet of Spinalonga**, re-named Kalydonia in 1945. The etymology of the name Spinalonga is interesting: it is the Italian for 'long thorn'. But the Venetians did not give the island this name because it looked like a long thorn: the name is actually a corruption of the Greek 'stin Elounta' as heard by Italian ears. It was here that the Venetians built in 1579, on the ruins of the ancient acropolis, a strong fortress to protect the Gulf of Mirabello. This was one of the few anywhere in Crete which did not fall into the hands of the Turks when they conquered Crete in 1669, but remained in the possession of the Venetians. In 1903, by a decision of the autonomous republic of Crete, Spinalonga became a colony for the lepers of Crete, which it remained until 1957. Today the island is a tourist centre with large numbers of vistors. Spinalonga can be reached by caïque from **Ayios Nikolaos**, **Elounta** and **Plaka**. As we continue to the north along the coast road, we come to cosmopolitan **Elounta** (10.5 km. from Ayios Nikolaos), one of Greece's most popular tourist resorts. The name comes from the ancient city of Olous, which stood on the isthmus which used to link the headland with the island. The Commune of Elounta is made up of five villages, of which only Schisma is on the sea, and so attracts all the visitors. Our next stop is **Plaka**, a beautiful fishing-village with a picturesque little harbour, some 5 km. from Elounta. In order to continue with our route, we go back to Elounta and take the turning to the left which leads into the interior of the Prefecture. After 10 km., we reach the attractive and fertile vil-

p. 174

Above: View of the seaside village of Elounda.

Below: Spinalonga, opposite Elounda. The fortress which can be seen on the islet is Venetian (1579).

lage of **Fourni**, from which a poor road leads to the **Areti Monastery**, which stands in a wood at a height of 530 metres. Back on the main road, we start to go downhill, leaving on the left the pretty village of **Nikithiano**, with its windmills and on the right Ayios Antonios hill, topped by a chapel dedicated to St Antony, and take the old national road, which passes through Neapolis and brings us to the village of **Latsida** (at 18 km.). From here we can visit the village of **Milatos,** with the historic **Milatos cave**. **Minoan Milatos** stood between the village and the sea. If we take the road to the west from Milatos, we come to **Epano Sisi** and the seaside village of **Sisi**. From this point we return to the old national road and go through the Varchasi gorge to visit the **chapel of St George 'Selinaris'** (on the right of the Mt Selena gorge) and the attractive village of **Vrachasi**. The return to Ayios Nikolaos can be made by either the old or the new national road, after passing through the **Limnes** with its mills, a village built in the traditional style.

Longer routes

3. Ayios Nikolaos - Neapoli - Plain of Lasithi

From Ayios Nikolaos we take the national road in the direction of Herakleio, and, having crossed the Mirabello plain, we come, at 15 km., to Neapoli, which combines commerce with beauty, in a valley green with olive trees and orchards. South-west of Neapoli is the **Kremasta Monastery**. As we leave Neapoli, we take the road to the left and, having passed through the village of **Vryses** and the **Drasi valley**, we begin to climb, passing through **Amy-**

p. 177
Vignette from the life of Crete's farmers and shepherds, from the picturesque plain of Lasithi with its 10,000 windmills.

dali, **Apano** and **Kato Zenia**, **Exo Potami**, and **Mesa Potami**, until we come to the point known as 'tou Patera ta Sellia' at 1100 metres. We now have the **Plain of Lasithi** spread out before us. The area is irrigated by thousands of water pumps, which make a striking sight. This little paradise covers 2,500 hectares and is at a height of 850 metres, and the plain itself is a sub-prefecture with 21 villages and 12 communes. We come to the first of these after 30 km.: **Mesa Lasithi** (altitude 870 metres), where we can begin a tour of the plain which includes the villages of **Marmaketo** and **Farsaro** and the town of **Tzermiado**, capital of the sub-prefecture of Lasithi. At the eastern end of the town is the **Kastellos hill**, where, at **Skafida** and **Kastellos**, Neolithic graves and houses of the second Early Minoan period were first found in Crete. The road then passes through

p. 178

A glimpse of farming life in Crete.

the villages of **Lagou** and **Pinakiano**, and then **Kato Metochi**, **Ayios Haralambos** and **Plati**, all three built in the traditional style. After we have left Plati, but before reaching **Psychro**, we come to the tourist pavilion where it is possible to hire donkeys to take visitors, in about 15 minutes, to the entrance of the **Dictaean Cave**, on the northern side of Mt Dikti, at a height of 1025 metres. According to mythology, it was here that Zeus was born, before being taken to the Idaean Cave to be nurtured by the goat Amaltheia under the protection and supervision of the Kouretes shepherds. The cave was a place of worship from the Minoan to the Archaic period. The first part of the cave, used for sacrifices, had a small sanctuary and an altar. Steps lead to the second part, which is 65 metres lower. Here large numbers of stone votive tablets belonging to the Minoan and

p. 179

Tzermiado. The stone windmills lend individual colour to the region.

p. 181 ➤

Aerial photograph of Ierapetra, the southernmost city of Greece.

Mycenaean periods were found. Our tour of the Plain of Lasithi is completed by a visit to the village of **Psychro** (which takes its name - 'Chilly' - from the low temperatures to be encountered here)) and then the large **village of Ayios Georgios**. Here the **Cretan Folklore Museum** is worth visiting. From here a climb to **'Spathi'** on the highest peak (2148 metres) of Mt Dikti is a possibility. From **Drasi** we make the return to Ayios Nikolaos, following the road to the right, passing through the old-fashioned villages of **Exo Lakonia**, **Fioretzides** and **Flamouriana**.

4. Ayios Nikolaos - visit to the archaeological site of Gournia - Pacheia Ammos - Ierapetra - Makryialos - Kapsas - Myrtos - Anatoli - Istros

p. 180

The archaeological site of Gournia. Its largest building - the 'palace' - was excavated at the highest point of the hill.

We leave Ayios Nikolaos by the coast road to Ierapetra and Siteia. Before we come to Gournia, we can visit the **Faneromeni Monastery**, which takes the form of a two-aisled church in a cave. **The archaeological site of Gournia** contains the remains of a large Minoan settlement with houses, roads and a large building on the top of the hill, which was probably the residence of the city's ruler. Also of interest is a small sanctuary with a wealth of votive tablets and other sacred objects. What this place was called in an-

p. 183 ▶

Istros.

tiquity is not known. It was given the name 'Gournia' ('hollows') by the local people because of the large number of small hollows in the stone which could be seen among the half-buried ruins before the excavations took place. We continue eastwards on the road to Siteia and pass through the beautiful seaside village of **Pacheia Ammos**, which, standing on a picturesque natural harbour, is a junction for communications between Ierapetra and Siteia. Between Pacheia Ammos and Siteia is Crete's narrowest point. A road to the right goes off to Ierapetra, passing through **Episkopi**, the highest point on our route, and **Kato Chorio**, with its abundant running water. **Ierapetra**, the most southerly city in the whole of Greece, stands on the site of the ancient Hierapytna and today is a modern country town. The location of Ierapetra, on the

p. 182-183

The Makriyalos beach.

south coast of Crete, almost opposite Cyrenaica, has determined its history. In Roman times it was very prosperous. In the early thirteenth century it was taken by the Genoese, who built fortifications, still visible today. It next passed into the hands of the Venetians. The city's **Archaeological Museum**, which is housed in a municipal building in the central square, is worth a visit, as are the town's fine churches. The beaches on the **islet of Chrysi**, to the south, are ideal for relaxation.

To the east of Ierapetra a short trip brings us to the village of Ayia Fotia, the attractive seaside village of **Makryialos**, on the Bay of Kala Nera, and the village of **Analypsi**, from which we can visit the **seaside Kapsas Monastery**. From this point we can continue north to Siteia. If, however, we choose to leave Ierapetra in a westerly direction along the

p. 184

The beach at Ayia Fotia.

coast road, we come to **Myrtos**, a picturesque seaside village standing on the banks of the Kryo river. The village has a museum, housed in the prima-
ry school building, with pottery from different periods of Minoan civilisation, ceramics and sculpture
from Roman times, coins, weapons and folklore
items. A little before Myrtos, we encounter an important Early Minoan building with more than 24
rooms, a sanctuary and an interesting pottery work-
shop. We continue north-west towards Herakleio;
alternatively we can return to Ierapetra and take the
road off from the village of **Gra-Lyghia** to go up to
the charming village of **Anatoli**. Here there is another branch off the road. To the left we can reach
the **Xakousti Monastery**, the village of **Malles** (the
largest village in the Ierapetra area under Venetian
rule) and **Christos**. If we take the road to the right
in Anatoli, we come to **Istros**, and from there we
can return to Ayios Nikolaos.

5. Ayios Nikolaos - Mouliana - Hamezi - Siteia - Ayia Fotia - Toplou Monastery - Vaï - Itanos - Palaikastro - Kato Zakros

For the purposes of this route we leave Ayios Nikolaos by the coast road to Siteia. At the 26th kilometre, in a valley with olive trees, we come to the village of **Kavousi**. From there, we begin the ascent of
Mt Kapsas. Passing through the **Lastros valley**, we
reach the village of **Sfaka**, from which it is possible
to go down to the fishing-village of **Mochlos** or take
a trip to the islands of **Ayios Nikolaos** and **Pseira**.
If we continue to climb towards Sfaka, we come to
the village of **Tourloti**, which stands on the top of
Kastri hill. To the south of the village, on Kastri hill
(450 metres), there are remains of a Minoan settle-

ment. We then pass through the villages of **Myrsi-ni**, **Mesa** and **Exo Mouliana** and the charming village of **Hamezi**, on the south side of which the so-called 'Oval House', of the Middle Minoan period and looking like a fortress, was discovered. The village has a **Museum of Folk Art**, housed in a medieval building. From Hamezi we start to descend. The road passes through the village of **Skopi** and brings us, at the 70th kilometre, to Siteia, the birthplace of the poet Vincenzo Cornaros. The city forms an amphitheatre on the slopes of a low hill. It lies on the western side of the bay of **Siteia**, on the site

of the ancient Eteia, a city which Stephen of Byzantium says was the home of Myson, one of the Seven Sages of ancient Greece. Siteia is the most easterly city in Crete, the capital of its own sub-prefecture. Although it has developed as a tourist resort in recent years, it has retained much of the character and the social and economic life of earlier times. To the east is the **Frourio tou Kastrou**, known today as **Kazarma** (from 'Casa di Arma), the most imposing monument from the past to dominate present-day Siteia. This was either a barracks for the guard or military headquarters, one of the buildings, that

p. 186 - 187

The seaside town of Siteia. The fortress of Kastro, known as 'Kazarma' (Casa di Arma) can also be seen.

p. 189 ➤

'Great Art Thou, O Lord', icon by Ioannis Kornaros (1770) from the Toplou Monastery.

p. 188

Toplou Monastery. The interior is adorned with well-preserved wall-paintings of the fourteenth century and important portable icons of the famous Cretan School.

is, of medieval Siteia, which was walled.

The town's **Archaeological Museum** contains items which illustrate the history and culture of the ancient city, while the small **Folklore Museum**, which is on the first floor of an old house, has collections of textiles, embroideries, local costumes and other examples of folk art and crafts. The airport, with flights to and from Athens, is to the north of the town. If we travel eastwards from Siteia, we come first to the seaside village of **Ayia Fotia**. The whole area around the village is of great archaeological interest: apart from various chance finds and traces of habitation in the **Koufotos cave**, on the coast, a vast necropolis of the Early Minoan period was found at **Patela**, near the cave, with 252 graves.

If we now take the road off to the left, we come to the historic **Toplou Monastery**, which looks like a fortress and stands in wild and rugged country at the base of the Kavo Sideris headland. This historic

59

monastery was one of the largest and richest in Crete. Its name is Turkish and means a cannon ball and it acquired it because of the cannon which it possessed under Turkish occupation to ward off pirates. It is also known by the name of Our Lady Akrotiriani ('of the headland'). Square in shape, it is surrounded by a wall and covers an area of 800 sq. m. The walls of its church are decorated with well-preserved paintings of the fourteenth century. Among its portable icons is the 'Great art Thou, O Lord' by Ioannis Kornaros, made up of miniatures of biblical scenes and a masterpiece of Cretan art. In 1821, the Turks massacred 12 monks in the Monastery's vaulted entrance, the so-called loggia gate, and it was left abandoned. In 1866, the Turkish army again laid waste the Monastery. If we continue north-east from Toplou Monastery, we come to **Vaï**. This famous little bay with its fine sand is ringed by a wood of date-palm trees. This wood is open to the public only between dawn and sunset. This 'African' landscape, a little oasis for relaxation, attracts many visitors.

If we return to our original route, we can continue north to the attractive **Ermoupoli bay**, the site of ancient **Itanos**, named after one of the Kouretes who brought up Zeus. Excavations have shown that the city was inhabited from the Minoan period to the fifteenth century AD, when it was destroyed by pirates. We can now go back to **Palaiokastro**, which was inhabited from the Minoan to the Hellenistic period. At **Rousolakkos** another settlement, this time of the Middle Minoan period, was discovered and various finds have shown that this was the site of a sanctuary dedicated to Dictaean Zeus. On **Petsofa** hill, south of Palaiokastro, an

p. 191
View of part of the famous palm grove of Vaï and the fine beach, which attracts a host of visitors.

open-air sanctuary of the Middle Minoan period which yielded important finds (such as figurines in an attitude of prayer) was found. It would seem that some god or goddess of healing was invoked here by those afflicted with various illnesses.

From here, an uphill road brings us to **Epano Zakros**, one of the most picturesque villages on Crete. It stands on two hills and has a wealth of olive and fruit trees. Eight kilometres to the east, near a very fine beach, are the remains of a small seaside settlement, on the western edge of which a Minoan palace was discovered. This is the fourth largest Minoan palace to come to light in Crete and the most recently discovered. Naturally, it must have owed its existence to its important geographical position. S-

tanding on a safe inlet on the south coast of the island, it provided the main access to the cultures of the East. It was built in c. 1600 BC and destroyed around 1450, like the rest of the palaces, by a severe earthquake, perhaps the one which, with its associated volcanic eruptions, caused a part of the island of Thera (Santorini) to sink beneath the waves, and it is a fact that ash of volcanic origin mingled with sulphur was found near the palace. This palace, of an area of 8,000 sq. m., is one-fifth of the size of the palace of Knossos, but it is laid out in a way similar to the rest of the palaces: there is a central paved courtyard (with three entrances to the west, with an altar in front of the main one) around which the building is laid out. It was in this central

p. 192 - 193

Aerial photograph of Vaï with its grove of palm trees, unique in Greece.

open-air area, which was surrounded by grandiose facades and small colonnades with columns and timber beams, that religious rites took place, as is shown by the remains of a small altar, loaded with votive items. On the western side were the quarters for the officials, on the east, the main apartments, and on the south, the workshops. We enter from the east and follow a paved road, known as the 'port road' and come on the left to the remains of a foundry, unique for its period, with the kiln and four air-vents leading to an oval room with a hole and a trap-door, where the metal was channeled towards circular hollows outside the foundry. Also of interest are the so-called Hall of Ceremonies, the Banquet Hall, decorated with a band of spirals in relief, the sanctuary, the storerooms, and a circular basin in which olives - 3,500 years old and perfectly preserved in the water - were found together with other materials of plant origin. The Minoan palaces had a double function: they were centres of worship of the deity and the palace of the king. Excavations in this area have also uncovered four large Minoan farmhouses, two mountain-top shrines, cemeteries and burial caves belonging to the Minoan and Early Greek periods. Above the valley a grave precinct was recently discovered, while fresh excavations have brought to light, on the eastern edge of a small inner courtyard, an imposing building, contemporary with the palace of Knossos, which was without doubt the first palace of Kato Zakros. Digs have also been carried out below the central court of the great palace and have revealed the existence of a courtyard underground, which must have belonged to the first palace.

p. 195 ▶

A & B: View of the archaeological site of Zakro. The palace which was discovered here was built c.1600 BC and was destroyed around 1450 BC.

We return to **Palaiokastro** and from there we can make our way back to Siteia and Ayios Nikolaos.

Prefecture of Chania

Access to the Prefecture

There are daily sailings from Chania to the port of Piraeus: these ships dock at Souda Bay, 157 nautical miles from Piraeus (a distance which is covered in about 10 hours). Town buses cover the 7 km. route from Chania to the dock on Souda Bay. There are also sailings twice a week from Piraeus to Kastelli Kissamou via Monemvasia, Neapoli and Yitheio (in the Peloponnese) and the islands of Kithira (Ayia Pelagia and Kapsali) and Antikithira. The last stage of the journey takes about six hours. There are regular flights to Athens from the airport at Akrotiri (15.2 km. from Chania); departures are frequent in the summer and less so in the winter. The flight takes 45 minutes. There are also flights (in 1 hour 15 minutes) from Chania to Thessaloniki.

Telephone numbers

Piraeus Harbourmaster's Office: tel. nos 210/417.2657, 411.4785
Chania Harbourmaster's Office: tel. no. 28210/28.888
Kastelli Port Office: tel. no. 28220/22.024
Olympic Airways office in Athens: tel. no. 966.6666.
Olympic Airways office in Thessaloniki: tel. no. 2310/281.880
Olympic Airways office in Chania: tel. no. 28210/57.701-3
Olympic Airways office at Chania airport: tel. no. 63.264, 63.171
Civil Aviation Authority: tel. no. 63.264

Travelling around the Prefecture

Town buses, Olympic Airways coaches and taxis serve the route from the airport to Chania. Inside the Prefecture, there are KTEL buses to all the villages, and small boats run along the south coast and from there to Gavdos. The roads of the Prefecture are good, most of the access routes to the south coast being surfaced. There are local sailings from Chora Sfakion to Loutro, Ayia Roumeli, Souyia and Palaiochora and out to the island of Gavdos. Boats also run from Palaiochora and Souyia to Gavdos. Trips to the sights in the Prefecture are organised by various travel agencies. Car and moped hire agencies are to be found in abundance in Chania, in Souda, at the airport and in many of the villages, and there is no shortage of taxis.

Telephone numbers:
Chora Sfakion Port Office: tel. no. 28250/91.292
Palaiochora Port Office: tel. no. 28230/41.214
KTEL bus station: tel. nos. 23.052, 23.306

Local products

Chania has a wide range of shops selling folk art products, jewellery and leather goods. Of particular interest are the shops which sell *stivánia,* the traditional tall leather boots. Throughout the Prefecture visitors will find local cheese, *raki* and honey. Chestnuts from Ennea Choria, Kissamou, are a special treat.

INFORMATION - SOME USEFUL TELEPHONE NOS:

Area code 28210
Greek National Tourist
Organisation 92.943
Chania Town Hall 97.777
Chania Police Headquarters 51.111
Souda Police Station 89.316
Chania Traffic Police 41.111
Chania Harbour Police 45.117
Souda Harbour Police 89.240
ELPA motorists' assistance 104
Express Service motorists'
assistance 154
Hellas Service motorists'
assistance 157
Chania Fire Brigade 199
First Aid Centre 166
Hospital 22.222
Chania Red Cross 22.550
Naval Hospital, Souda 89.307-9
Chania Health Centre 52.798
Souda Customs House 89.277
Chania Customs House 57.769

Prefecture of Rethymno

Access to the Prefecture

There are regular ferry sailings all the year round from Rethymno to Piraeus, which is 160 nautical miles away. The voyage takes about 12 hours. There are also connections by air for Athens and Thessaloniki via Chania airport.

Telephone numbers

Piraeus Harbourmaster's Office: tel. no. 210/417.2657
Rethymno Harbourmaster's Office: tel. no. 28310/28.971
Olympic Airways, Rethymno: tel. no. 28310/22.257
Olympic Airways, Chania: tel. no. 28210/57.701

Moving around the Prefecture

Chania airport is 68 km. from Rethymno and passengers make the connection on the Olympic Airways coach or by KTEL bus. In summer, there are two cruise liner sailings per week from Rethymno to Santorini. Caiques sail from Ayia Galini for Matala in the Prefecture of Herakleio and from Plakias for Ayios Pavlos, Ayia Galini and Preveli. In the hinterland of the Prefecture, town and long-distance KTEL buses connect Rethymno with the nearer and more distant villages and beaches. There are also a number of taxis. Cars and mopeds may be rented in Rethymno itself and in many of the towns and villages.

Telephone numbers:
KTEL bus station: tel. no. 22.212

Local products

Cheese of the highest quality *(graviéra, myzíthra* and *anthótyro)* may be bought in Rethymno and in the mountain villages. Rethymno itself is well-known for its woven goods and embroideries (woven goods can also be obtained in Anoyeia and Zoniana). There are folk art shops selling leather goods, copperware, ornamental pottery and wood-carvings. The town also has a number of jewellers' shops. Pure honey is on sale in the village of Margarites, as is good pottery: there are local studios. Outstanding fruit and cheese can be bought in the villages of the Amari valley.

INFORMATION - SOME USEFUL TELEPHONE NOS:

Area code 28310
Greek State Tourist
Organisation...71.227
Rethymno Town Hall.............................22.245
Tourist Police...28.156
Police -
Emergency Service...................................100
Rethymno Police Headquarters.............22.238
Rethymno Traffic Police.........................22.589
Rethymno Harbour Police 22.276
Rethymno Customs House 22.292, 24.458
ELPA motorists' assistance 104
Express Service motorists'
assistance...154
Hellas Service motorists'
assistance...157
Rethymno Fire Brigade...........................199
First Aid Centre 166
Hospital 27.491
Rethymno IKA
(medical services) 22.400

Prefecture of Herakleio

Access to the Prefecture

The Prefecture of Herakleio can be reached by ferry from the port of Piraeus. There are frequent sailings in summer - fewer in winter. The ferry takes 12 hours to cover the 174 nautical miles between the two ports. There is also a ferry between Herakleio and Thessaloniki, while there are ferry services to many of the islands of the Aegean, particularly (in summer) the Cyclades. There is also a service which starts from Venice, calls at Herakleio and then Limassol, and goes to Haifa in Israel. Herakleio can be reached by air: in summer there are frequent flights from Athens (approximately 50 minutes) and Thessaloniki (approximately 1 hour, 15 minutes). There is also a service all the year round linking the city with Rhodes and in high season with Mykonos. There are, of course, many charter flights in summer from many cities of Europe.

Telephone numbers

Piraeus Harbourmaster's Office: tel. nos 210/411.4785, 417.2657
Herakleio Harbourmaster's Office: tel. nos 2810/244.956, 244.912
Thessaloniki Harbourmaster's Office: tel. no 2310/531.505
Olympic Airways, Athens: tel. no. 210/966.6666
Olympic Airways, Herakleio: tel. no. 2810/229.191
Olympic Airways at Herakleio airport: tel. no. 245.644
Olympic Airways, Thessaloniki: tel. no. 2310/281.880

Travelling around the Prefecture

Herakleio airport is 4.8 km to the east of the city and can be reached by Olympic Airway buses or by taxi. There are good and frequent bus services to every part of the Prefecture. Car and motorbike hire agencies can be found in Herakleio, at the airport

and in many villages which are popular with tourists.
Telephone numbers: *Bus Services:* tel. no. 2810/221.765

Local products

Agricultural products can be purchased throughout the Prefecture. These include olive oil, wine, tsikoudia (marc brandy), olives, currants, fruit, honey, herbs, local sausages and a variety of excellent cheeses. In the shops catering for tourists traditional ceramic and bronze artefacts, local hand-woven textiles and embroideries can be found. In Herakleio, in Kalokairinou Avenue and 1821 Street and elsewhere in the city, the traditional craft of knife-making is still practised. There are also shops in the city which sell leather goods and high-quality reproductions of items of ancient jewellery in the island's museums.

INFORMATION - USEFUL TELEPHONE NOS

Area code	2810
Greek State Tourist Organisation - Hotels Section	228.203
Tourist Police	283.190
Irakleio Town Hall	227.102, 227.124
Municipal Police	289.900
Irakleio Police Headquarters	282.241
Irakleio Traffic Police	282.031
Irakleio Harbour Police	226.073
ELPA motorists' assistance	104
Express Service motorists' assistance	154
Hellas Service motorists' assistance	157
Irakleio Fire Brigade	199
First Aid Centre	222.222
Hospital ('Venizelio')	237.502
University Hospital	269.111
'Apollonian' Hospital	229.713
IKA (medical services)	287.220
Customs House (Irakleio Harbour)	246.200
Customs House (Irakleio Airport)	220.390

Prefecture of Lasithi

Access to the Prefecture

Ayios Nikolaos and Siteia can be reached by ferry from Piraeus. Sailings are frequent in summer. The distance from Piraeus to Ayios Nikolaos is 200 nautical miles (approximately 12 hours) and to Siteia 206 nautical miles (approximately 13 hours). They can also be reached by air from Athens via the airports of Herakleio and Siteia (flight time: approximately 1 hour 20 minutes).

Telephone numbers

Piraeus Harbourmaster's Office: tel. nos 210/417.2657, 411.4785
Ayios Nikolaos Harbourmaster's Office: tel. no. 28410/22.312
Siteia Port Office: tel. no. 28430/22.310
Olympic Airways, Athens: tel. no. 210/966.6666
Olympic Airways, Siteia: tel. no. 28430/22.270
Olympic Airways at Siteia airport: tel. no. 28430/24.666

Travelling around the Prefecture

The airport is 1 km. from the town and can be reached by taxi, local buses and the Olympic Airways bus. The Lasithi-based bus services provide transport between the three main towns (Ayios Nikolaos, Siteia, Ierapetra) and most of the villages of the Prefecture, as well as to Herakleio, Rethymno and Chania. It is possible to take boat trips from Ayios Nikolaos and Elounta to the islet of Spinalonga and from Ierapetra to the islet of Chrysi in the Libyan Sea. Hire cars and motorbikes are available in Ayios Nikolaos, Siteia, Elounta, Ierapetra and most places favoured by visitors. There is also a plentiful supply of taxis.

Telephone numbers:
Ayios Nikolaos bus services: tel. no. 28410/22.234
Ierapetra bus services: tel. no. 28420/28.237

Local products

In all the large towns there are shops which sell the products of Cretan folk art. The standards of taste are high. Attractive textiles, embroideries and small wood carvings can be found at Kritsa, while Ayia Fotia produces honey of exceptional quality. A wide range of high-quality jewellery can be purchased in Ayios Nikolaos.

INFORMATION - USEFUL TELEPHONE NOS

Area code, Ayios Nikolaos	28410
Greek State Tourist Organisation	22.357
Police (Ayios Nikolaos Emergency Service)	100
Police Station	22251
Tourist Police	22.321
Ayios Nikolaos Traffic Police	22.750
ELPA motorists' assistance	104
Express Service motorists' assistance	154
Hellas Service motorists' assistance	157
First Aid Centre	166
Hospital	22.369, 22011

IERAPETRA

Area code	28420
Police	22560
Tourist Police	24.200
Hospital	22.488

SITEIA

Area code	28430
Tourist Police	24.200
Hospital	22.347

PREFECTURE OF CHANIA - HOTELS

TOWN / AREA CATEGORY	NAME	TEL. No.	No. of BEDS
AGIA MARINA (28210)			
B	AMALTHIA	68.542	115
B	ATRION	68.636	102
B	CANEA MARE	68.825	97
B	MINERVA BEACH	68.813	41
B	SANTA MARINA	68.570	120
B	SKALA	68.680	16
C	ACITION	68.922	59
C	ALEXIA BEACH	68.110	41
C	ANTIGONE	68.106	23
C	APLADAS	68.700/3	132
C	ARCHITECT'S VILLAS II	68.526	18
C	BELLA VISTA VILLAGE	68.100	50
C	ELOTIS	68.622	52
C	EROFILI	68.529	33
C	GLAROS	68.747	68
C	IOLIDA	60.821	53
C	IOLIDA II	60.821	24
C	MANIAS	55.401	24
C	MARINA SANDS	68.691/4	45
C	OSCAR	68.773	99
C	RELAX	68.806	70
C	SANTA MARINA II	68.460	90
C	STEFAN VILLAGE	—	86
C	TA THODOROU	68.510	14
AGIA ROUMELI (28210)			
C	AGHIA ROUMELI	25.657	13
C	CRI-CRI	—	24
AGII APOSTOLI (28210)			
C	APTERA BEACH	22.636	92
C	CALYPSO	32.013	55
C	FLAMINGOS		56
AGIOS IOANNIS (28210)			
B	NOTOS	54.278	64
ALMIRIDA (28250)			
L	ALMIRIDA	—	70
A	DIMITRA	—	70
B	ALMIRIDA BAY	31.751	93
C	ALMIRA	—	14

TOWN / AREA CATEGORY	NAME	TEL. No.	No. of BEDS
DARATSOS (28210)			
A	STAR DARATSOS	—	32
B	ALTHEA VILLAGE	31.320	120
B	GOLDEN BAY	—	56
B	KARAVANOS	32.315	23
B	MALOU	32.332	24
B	SIRIOS VILLAGE	32.102	189
C	ASTRA	32.302	29
C	CLEO	32.326	25
C	DREAM LAND	—	51
C	GOLDEN SAND	32.351/3	66
C	LOTUS	31.660	40
C	NANA	—	40
C	TALOS	28.682	31
DRAMIA (28310)			
C	MARI	61.569	58
ELOS VATHI (28220)			
C	AGIOS DIKAEOS	61.275	17
GALATAS (28210)			
A	PANORAMA	31.700/6	309
C	BALITO	—	36
C	CRETA MARIA	51.335	29
C	DAFNI	32.101	35
C	GIANNIS-ELENI		46
C	KORINNA	31.767	33
C	VACHOS	68.526	44
C	VENUS	32.110	17
C	VILLA ANASTASIA	31.413	20
C	VILLA ARMONIA	22.746	18
C	ZOTIS	32.413	34
GEORGIOUPOLI (28250)			
A	MARE MONTE	61.390	195
A	PILOT BEACH	61.002/3	194
A	VANTARIS BEACH	—	102
C	DROSSIA	61.326	23
C	GORGONA	61.341	79
C	KORISSIA	61.389	44
C	LAVYRINTHOS	61.373	38
C	MITHOLOGY	61.414	51
C	MONTREAL	—	36
C	NIKITAS	—	14

PREFECTURE OF CHANIA - HOTELS

TOWN / AREA CATEGORY	NAME	TEL. No.	No. of BEDS
C	NOSTALGIE	61.327	43
C	TARRA	—	30

GERANI (28210)

A	CRETA PARADISE BEACH	61.315	184
C	IANTHIA	—	47

GERMANIKO POULI (28210)

C	AGAPI	27.410	17
C	PHAEDRA	25.752	21

HALEPA (28210)

B	ROYAL SUN	42.618	42

HANIA (28210)

A	AMFORA	93.224	42
A	CAPTAIN VASSILIS	51.122	13
A	CONTESSA	98.565	14
A	DOGIS	57.600	18
A	KYDON	52.280/4	191
A	PALAZZO	43.255	25
A	PANDORA	43.588/9	28
A	PORTO DEL COLOMBO	70.945	15
B	AKALI MELATHRON	41.000/4	152
B	ARCADI	90.181/2	109
B	BOZZALI	50.824	15
B	CASA DELFINO	93.098	31
B	CASA VENETA	90.074	23
B	DOLPHIN II APARTMENTS	44.434	38
B	DOMA	51.772/3	56
B	DOMENICO	55.019	10
B	EL GRECO	90.432	25
B	HALEPA	53.544/6	94
B	ILIANTHOS	20.828	11
B	KAROLOS STUDIOS	55.019	6
B	MARILY	95.589	9
B	MONTE VARDIA	40.872	38
B	NOSTOS	54.833	27
B	PORTO VENEZIANO	59.311/13	108
B	SAMARIA	71.271/5	110
B	VILLA ANDROMEDA	45.263/4	24
B	XENIA	91.238/9	88
C	AKROTIRI	54.669	26
C	AMPHITRITI	56.470/1	20
C	ARIS	—	21
C	ARTEMIS	23.035	10

TOWN / AREA CATEGORY	NAME	TEL. No.	No. of BEDS
C	ASTOR	55.557/8	68
C	CANDIA	91.943	33
C	CANEA	91.360/62	94
C	DANAOS	96.021/2	51
C	DIKTYNNA	51.103	61
C	ELENA	95.516	13
C	ELOTIA	—	59
C	FALASARNA	93.736/9	56
C	FALIRO	41.905	17
C	HELLINIS	28.070	28
C	IRENE	54.203	39
C	IRIDA	50.444	33
C	KRITI	51.881/5	189
C	KYDONIA	57.561/3	68
C	LATO	56.944	51
C	LIVA	45.310/11	37
C	LUCIA	91.843	72
C	NEFELI	70.007	65
C	OMALOS	95.215/7	63
C	ZEROS	44.921/3	34

KALAMAKI (28210)

C	AKASTI	31.352	64
C	ALEXANDRA	32.055	19
C	ARIADNI	31.484	32

KALATHAS (28210)

B	GIORGI'S BLUE APTS	64.080	36
B	LENA-AKTI	64.750	59
B	WATER LILY	64.755	26
C	APOLLO VILLA APARTMENTS	—	28
C	AREA	69.002	18
C	ARION	57.388	24
C	KRINI	64.795	21
C	SUNRISE	64.214	21
C	TZANAKAKI BEACH	64.363/5	68
C	VILLA KRINI	58.265	21

KALIVES (28250)

B	MAISTRALI	—	42
C	KALIVES BEACH	31.285	57

KAMISSIANA (28240)

B	KASTALIA	22.268	58
C	DIOM'S STUDIOS	22.376	26

PREFECTURE OF CHANIA - HOTELS

TOWN / AREA CATEGORY	NAME	TEL. No.	No. of BEDS
KANDANOS (28230)			
C	APOPIGADI	22.566/7	38
KATO GERANI (28210)			
C	ALFA	—	56
KATO STALOS (28210)			
C	ALCYON	68.021	38
C	ATLANTIS BEACH	68.537	51
C	CASA LOMA	68.689	29
C	DOLFIN	68.507	44
C	ESPERIDES	68.672	36
C	KATO STALOS	68.120/1	22
C	KOURMOULIS STUDIOS	68.804	29
C	PAVLAKIS BEACH	68.309	26
C	SEA SIDE	68.778	43
C	TROPIKANA BEACH	68.787	51
KAVROS (28250)			
C	HAPPY DAYS BEACH	61.201/2	130
C	ORFEAS BEACH	61.008	31
C	SOFIA	—	43
KISSAMOS (28220)			
B	HELENA BEACH	23.300/4	75
B	VILLA ARTEMIS DI	23.035	10
C	CASTLE	22.140/1	21
C	DIMITRIS-CHRYSSANI	23.390	40
C	HOLIDAYS	23.488	10
C	KISSAMOS	22.086	29
C	OLYMPIC	22.483	64
C	PELI	22.343	56
C	PERGAMOS VILLAGE	22.944/5	60
C	VAI	22.790	24
KOLIMBARI (28240)			
B	APHAEA VILLAGE	23.344/5	72
B	ARION	22.440	38
B	CHRYSSANA	22.812	78
C	ACROTIRI IRINIS FILIAS	22.485	19
C	AEOLOS	22.203	28
C	KOLYMBARI BEACH	22.725	146
C	LYKASTI	22.160	53
C	NIRIIDES	22.257	55
KORAKIES (28210)			
B	CORAKIES VILLAGE	64.584	34
KOUNOUPIDIANA (28210)			
C	LEONIDAS	64.472	32
C	PYRGOS	64.431	31
KOURNA (28250)			
C	KAVROS BEACH	61.322	155
C	MANOS BEACH	61.221	29
C	MINA	61.483	32
MALEME (28210)			
A	CRETE CHANDRIS	62.221/5	767
B	ALBATROS	—	62
C	FLISVOS	62.188	39
C	FUTURA	62.573	84
C	LEDRA	62.366	34
C	LEDRA MALEME	62.366	35
NEA KIDONIA (28210)			
B	ANAIS	32.202	32
C	ALEXIS	45.404	50
C	FORUM	32.425	106
C	GOLDEN BEACH	21.981	18
C	KEDRISSOS	71.500	47
C	KORINNA MARE	31.767	57
C	RAINBOW	31.810	34
OMALOS (28210)			
C	NEOS OMALOS	67.269	49
C	TO EXARI	—	46
PALEOHORA (28230)			
B	ELMAN	41.412/4	41
C	AGHAS	41.525	31
C	ARIS	41.502	56
C	DICTAMO	41.569	33
C	ELIROS	41.348	18
C	GLAROS	41.613	29
C	MEGIM	41.690	44
C	ON THE ROCKS	41.713	22

PREFECTURE OF CHANIA - HOTELS

CATEGORY	NAME	TEL. No.	No. of BEDS
C	PAL BEACH	41.512	104
C	POLYDOROS	41.068	24
C	REA	41.307	27

PERIVOLIA (28210)

CATEGORY	NAME	TEL. No.	No. of BEDS
A	OASSIS	94.829	24

PLATANIAS (28210)

CATEGORY	NAME	TEL. No.	No. of BEDS
B	GERANIOTIS BEACH	68.681/3	146
B	SANTA ELENA	—	134
C	ARCHIPELAGOS	—	46
C	DESPINA	68.807	59
C	ERATO	68.824	156
C	FILOXENIA	68.502	18
C	IDEAL BEACH	—	66
C	IFIGENIA	—	18
C	INDIGO MARE	—	101

CATEGORY	NAME	TEL. No.	No. of BEDS
C	KASTRO	48.583	99
C	KRONOS	68.630	89
C	RANIA	—	33
C	VAROUXAKIS	—	33
C	VILLA PLATANIAS	48.333	32

SFAKIA (28250)

CATEGORY	NAME	TEL. No.	No. of BEDS
B	VRITOMARTIS	91.222	161
C	PORTO LOUTRO	91.091	34
C	XENIA	91.238	23

SOUGIA (28230)

CATEGORY	NAME	TEL. No.	No. of BEDS
C	PIKILASSOS	51.242	19
C	SANTA IRENE	51.342	30

STAVROS (28210)

CATEGORY	NAME	TEL. No.	No. of BEDS
C	REA	39.001/4	83

PREFECTURE OF RETHYMNO - HOTELS

ADELE (28310)

CATEGORY	NAME	TEL. No.	No. of BEDS
A	RITHIMNA BEACH	29.491	1058
B	ADELE BEACH BUNG/WS	71.047	150
B	DIAS	71.017	100
B	EVA BAY	71.248	55
B	MARAVEL LAND	71.064	129
B	ORION	71.471/3	138
C	GOLDEN BEACH	71.012	200
C	GOLDEN SUN	71.284	74
C	KATERINA BEACH	71.270	116
C	MARAVEL	71.271	88
C	RINA	71.013	37

AGIA GALINI (28320)

CATEGORY	NAME	TEL. No.	No. of BEDS
B	SUNNINGDALE	91.161	36
C	ACROPOLIS	91.234	32
C	ADONIS	91.333/4	39
C	ADONIS II	91.334	52
C	ANDROMEDA	91.264	40
C	ARIADNI	91.380	12
C	ASTORIA	91.253	42
C	ATHINA	91.331	33

CATEGORY	NAME	TEL. No.	No. of BEDS
C	CANDIA	91.203	22
C	DEDALOS	91.214	24
C	EL GRECO	91.187	32
C	EROFILI	91.319	18
C	FEVRO	91.275	61
C	GALINI MARE	91.358	48
C	GHIOMA	91.190	25
C	GLAROS	91.151	52
C	IRINI MARE	91.488	69
C	IRO	91.160	21
C	NEOS IKAROS	91.447	19
C	OSTRIA	91.404	33
C	PETRA	91.155	49
C	PHAESTOS	91.223	16
C	REA	91.390	35
C	SELENA	91.273	15
C	SOULIA	91.307	22
C	STELLA	91.357	19
C	SUN LIGHT	91.286	44

BALI (28340)

CATEGORY	NAME	TEL. No.	No. of BEDS
A	BALI PARADISE	94.253/5	196
B	BALI BEACH	94.210/1	119

PREFECTURE OF RETHYMNO - HOTELS

CATEGORY	NAME	TEL. No.	No. of BEDS
TOWN / AREA			
B	TALEA BEACH	94.296/7	111
C	BALI MARE	—	65
C	BALI STAR	94.212	52
C	BALI VILLAGE	94.210	40
C	G. TROULIS	—	39

KALITHEA (28310)

CATEGORY	NAME	TEL. No.	No. of BEDS
B	LEFKONIKO BEACH	55.326/9	141
B	MINOS	24.173/6	254
C	PETRIS	22.465	42

KAMBOS PIGIS (28310)

CATEGORY	NAME	TEL. No.	No. of BEDS
A	EL GRECO	71.102	573
B	AMNISSOS	71.502	94

KERATIDES PRINOU (28310)

CATEGORY	NAME	TEL. No.	No. of BEDS
B	BEGIETIS BAY	71.909	114

KOUMBES (028310)

CATEGORY	NAME	TEL. No.	No. of BEDS
C	IRIS APARTMENTS	20.114	22

LEFKOGIA (28320)

CATEGORY	NAME	TEL. No.	No. of BEDS
C	AMMOUDI	31.355/6	50

MASTABAS (28310)

CATEGORY	NAME	TEL. No.	No. of BEDS
C	MARITA	26.991/2	51

MIRTHIO (28320)

CATEGORY	NAME	TEL. No.	No. of BEDS
A	DAMNONI RESORT	31.991/3	620
C	DAMMONI BAY	31.373	96

MISSIRIA (28310)

CATEGORY	NAME	TEL. No.	No. of BEDS
A	CRETA PALACE	21.181	714
B	DOMENICA	27.362	16
B	MAY	55.745	107
C	ANNA	22.590	30
C	APOLLON FIVOS	24.417	26
C	ARISTEA	—	24
C	EMILIA	21.029	24
C	ODISSIA BEACH	27.874	91
C	SEVEN BROTHERS	25.647	45
C	VENUS	55.300	29

PANORMOS (28340)

CATEGORY	NAME	TEL. No.	No. of BEDS
B	EUROPA	51.100	84

CATEGORY	NAME	TEL. No.	No. of BEDS
TOWN / AREA			
B	KIRKI	51.225	64
B	STELLA BEACH	—	65
B	VILLA KYNTHIA	51.102	14
C	ASTERION	51.081	24
C	KONAKI	51.386	48
C	PANORMO BEACH	51.321/3	61

PERIVOLIA (28310)

CATEGORY	NAME	TEL. No.	No. of BEDS
A	ATLANTIS BEACH	51.002	160
A	OLYMPIC II	24.766	27
B	BLUE SEA	54.804/5	43
B	IRENE	24.223	16
B	OASSIS	94.829	24
B	PEARL BEACH	51.513	167
C	ANITA BEACH	22.928	44
C	ARGO	—	41
C	BATIS	50.558/9	21
C	ELTINA	22.382	71
C	ERATO	26.913	31
C	FLISVOS BEACH STUDIOS	26.784	91
C	IVISKOS	51.112	162
C	KANTARAS	25.867	28
C	MELMAR	—	54
C	PLAZA	29.791	34
C	SILVER BEACH	71.136	100
C	THEO	29.769	31
C	ZANTINA BEACH	24.863	33

PLAKIAS (28320)

CATEGORY	NAME	TEL. No.	No. of BEDS
A	CALYPSO CRETIAN VILLAGE	31.296/7	204
B	NEOS ALIANTHOS	31.280/2	173
C	FLISVOS	31.421	21
C	LAMON	31.318	46
C	LIVYKON	31.216	27
C	LOFOS	31.422	27
C	MYRTIS	31.423	39
C	ORIZON BEACH	31.476	39
C	PHOENIX	31.331	30
C	PLAKIAS BAY	31.215	51
C	SKINARIA BEACH	31.295	93
C	SOPHIA BEACH	31.251/2	48
C	SUDA-MARE	31.931	33

PLATANES (28310)

CATEGORY	NAME	TEL. No.	No. of BEDS
A	LEONIKI	29.232	155
B	APP. KATERINI	—	42

PREFECTURE OF RETHYMNO - HOTELS

CATEGORY	NAME	TEL. No.	No. of BEDS
B	BUENO	25.554	48
B	MANDENIA	27.054	46
B	NEFELI	55.321/4	210
B	SANDY BEACH	26.993/4	82
B	STETHALI	25.551/3	44
C	APOLLON	—	108
C	ARIADNI	91.380	12
C	AXOS	23.513	104
C	GALEANA	29.553	123
C	MARINOS BEACH	27.840	114
C	TRYFON	24.772/4	60

PLATANIAS (28310)

CATEGORY	NAME	TEL. No.	No. of BEDS
B	CASTELLO BIANCO		66

RETHIMNO (28310)

CATEGORY	NAME	TEL. No.	No. of BEDS
A	ACHILLION PALACE	54.423	139
A	ADELE MARE	71.803/8	212
A	CRETA STAR	71.812	591
A	PALAZZO RIMONTI	51.289	42
A	PORTO RETHYMNO	50.432	369
A	RETHYMNO BAY	27.512/3	129
A	THE ARTEMIS PALACE	21.991	324
A	VYZANTIO	55.609	11
B	BELVEDERE	26.898	44
B	BRASCOS	23.721/3	156
B	ELEONORA	25.121/2	62
B	ELINA HOLIDAYS	27.395/7	40
B	FILOXENIA	21.345/6	71
B	FORTEZZA	55.551/2	102
B	GORTYNA	71.802	71
B	IDAEON	28.667/70	141
B	JASON	27.196	70
B	JO-AN	24.241/4	93
B	JOHN-MARI	51.368/9	62
B	KRITI BEACH	27.401/2	100
B	LIBERTY	21.851/3	45
B	MACARIS	20.280/3	169
B	MARDINIC	20.446	34
B	MYTHOS	53.917	26
B	OLYMPIC	24.761/4	123
B	PANTHEON	20.914	74
B	RETHEMNIOTIKO SPITI	23.923	19
B	ZANIA	28.169	12
B	ZORBAS BEACH	28.540	22
C	ADAM'S	20.905	18
C	AMBELI	21.233	14

CATEGORY	NAME	TEL. No.	No. of BEDS
C	ARCHIPELAGOS	54.757	92
C	ARMONIA	23.905	100
C	ASTALI	24.721/2	63
C	CAMARI GARDEN	31.272	76
C	DAISY	51.570	30
C	FOREST PARK	51.778	63
C	GREEN	22.225	17
C	ILIOS	21.672/4	124
C	IONIA	22.902	50
C	KONSTANTIN	20.221/2	40
C	KOSTIS	29.159	46
C	KYMA BEACH	21.503/4	64
C	LEON	26.197	25
C	LOGGETA	27.846	34
C	MAREM	28.759	56
C	MIRAMARE BEACH	24.118	45
C	PALLADION	71.789	94
C	PARK	29.958	18
C	PIGASSOS	25.530	51
C	PANORAMA	—	46
C	SAMARIA	53.925	44
C	STERIS BEACH	28.303	83
C	VALARI	22.236	42
C	VEKIO	54.985	56
C	VENETIA	25.092	13

ROUMELI MYLOPOTAMOU (28340)

CATEGORY	NAME	TEL. No.	No. of BEDS
B	GRECORAMA	51.070	150

SFAKAKI PAGALOHRIOU (28310)

CATEGORY	NAME	TEL. No.	No. of BEDS
C	EKAVI BEACH	71.896	78

SKALETA (28310)

CATEGORY	NAME	TEL. No.	No. of BEDS
A	RETHYMNO MARE	71.703	135
B	SKALETA BEACH	71.702	216
C	OASSIS	71.774	22

STAVROMENOS (28310)

CATEGORY	NAME	TEL. No.	No. of BEDS
C	ARSINIA	71.283	28
C	ASTRID	—	30
C	NIKI	71.038	22
C	PALVOS	71.304	32

XIROKAMARO (28310)

CATEGORY	NAME	TEL. No.	No. of BEDS
C	GEORGIANNA BEACH	71.503	94

PREFECTURE OF IRAKLEIO - HOTELS

CATEGORY	NAME	TEL. No.	No. of BEDS
AGIA PELAGIA (2810)			
A	ALEXANDER HOUSE	811.303	109
A	CAPSIS BEACH	811.112	1228
A	IRINI	—	12
A	PENINSULA	811.313	367
B	MONONAFTIS	811.213	74
B	PANORAMA	811.002	156
B	PERLA	811.012	49
B	STELIOS	811.071/2	76
C	ANATOLI	—	20
C	EVA MARE I	811.186	15
C	EVA MARE II	811.186	17
C	HARIS	—	58
AMNISSOS (2810)			
B	KARTEROS	228.802	105
C	PRINCE OF LILLIES	225.822	41
AMOUDARA (2810)			
A	AGAPI BEACH	250.502	391
A	AGAPI BEACH VIP	250.502	24
A	CRETA BEACH	252.302	262
A	DOLPHIN BAY	821.276/77	498
A	SANTA MARINA BEACH	261.103	220
B	AGAPI VILLAGE	250.502	141
B	LAMBI	821.124	135
B	MARILENA	254.312	116
C	ANGELA	250.660	22
C	GORGONA	821.920	73
C	LYKTOS	242.407	36
C	MINOAS	821.557	67
C	OSTRIA	—	14
C	SANTA ELENA	251.770/2	104
C	TSANGARAKIS BEACH	251.768	83
C	VIOLETTA	250.773	33
ARVI (28950)			
C	ARIADNI	71.300	22
GOURNES (2810)			
A	EVINA	761.034	62
B	ROYAL	245.412	126

CATEGORY	NAME	TEL. No.	No. of BEDS
C	ERATO	761.277	46
C	KRI-KRI VILLAGE	761.063	60
GOUVES (28970)			
A	APHRODITE BEACH	41.102	435
A	CRETA SUN	41.103	568
A	MAGDA	42.307/8	64
A	MARINA	41.361/2	728
A	PANTHEON PALACE	41.198	536
A	SWEET MEMORY	—	28
B	APOLLO	41.271	84
B	ASTIR BEACH	41.141	161
B	BYRON	41.130	49
B	CHRISTI APARTMENTS	—	72
B	MARIYANNA	—	54
C	CALYPSO HOLIDAYS	41.390	72
C	DESPO	41.353	67
C	DIOSCOURI	—	44
C	EDERI	41.204	50
C	GOUVES SEA	41.401	31
C	KAISSA BEACH	41.148	102
C	KOUROS	41.389	78
C	LAVRIS	41.101	181
C	MANIA	—	18
C	MON REPOS	41.280/5	90
C	SERENITE	—	15
C	SONIA	41.368	35
C	STUDIOS LIDA	41.456	21
HANI KOKINI (2810)			
A	ANNA	761.691	22
A	ARINA SAND	761.135	452
A	CORALI BEACH	—	42
A	KNOSSOS BEACH	761.204	206
A	MARY VILLAGE	—	26
A	RINELA BEACH	761.713	572
A	THEMIS BEACH	761.412	229
B	XENIA-ILIOS	761.524	205
C	AKTI	761.260	37
C	ARMILIDES	761.256	29
C	COSMAN	—	68
C	DANAE	761.375	34
C	DIONYSSOS	761.371	23
C	KAMARI	761.340	62

PREFECTURE OF IRAKLEIO - HOTELS

CATEGORY	NAME	TEL. No.	No. of BEDS
TOWN / AREA			
C	PRIMA	761.109	24
C	SUNSET	761.553	34

IRAKLIO (2810)

A	ASTORIA	229.002	273
A	ATLANTIS	229.103	296
A	FODELE BEACH	521.251/5	603
A	GALAXY	238.812	264
A	MINOA PALACE	380.404/6	230
A	XENIA	284.000/4	156
B	ATRION	229.225	117
B	ESPERIA	228.534	94
B	KASTRO	285.020	63
B	MEDITERRANEAN	289.331/4	105
B	PETRA	229.912	64
C	APOLLON	250.025	96
C	ARES	280.646	30
C	ATHINAIKON	229.312	77
C	BLUE SKY	254.612	50
C	CASTELLO	251.234	120
C	DAEDALOS	224.391	109
C	DOMENICO	228.703	73
C	EL GRECO	281.071/5	165
C	EVANS	223.928	48
C	GRABELLES	241.205/8	71
C	HERACLEION	281.881/3	72
C	ILAIRA	227.103	32
C	IRENE	226.561	105
C	KRETA	282.238	18
C	KRIS	223.211	17
C	KRONOS	282.240	28
C	LATO	228.103/5	99
C	MARIN	220.737	87
C	METROPOLE	244.280	71
C	MIRABELLO	285.052	42
C	OASSIS	254.082	35
C	OLYMPIC	288.861/4	135
C	SANTA ELENA	251.770/1	104
C	SELENA	226.377/8	52

KARTEROS (2810)

B	AMNISSOS	281.332/5	108
B	MOTEL XENIA	246.446	84
C	XENIOS DIAS	380.156	10

CATEGORY	NAME	TEL. No.	No. of BEDS
TOWN / AREA			

KOKINOS PIRGOS (28920)

B	FILIPPOS	52.002	86
C	LIBYAN SEA	51.621	42
C	LITTLE INN	51.400	87
C	MARY-ELEN	51.268	109
C	TA ADELFIA	51.462	20

LENTAS (28920)

C	LENTAS	95.221	23

LIMENAS HERSONISSOU (28970)

L	CRETA MARIS	22.115/30	1014
L	KNOSSOS ROYAL VILLAGE	23.575	661
L	PARADISE	22.893	82
A	ACROPOLIS	22.172	60
A	ANNISA BEACH	22.454	524
A	ANNABEL VILLAGE	23.561/4	398
A	ARLEN BEACH	—	20
A	ARTEMIS	23.570	36
A	ATHINA INN	23.765	32
A	BELVEDERE	22.010/5	547
A	CRETAN VILLAGE	22.295	442
A	CRISTI	—	20
A	EAST APARTMENTS	22.850/6	52
A	EUROPA BEACH	23.501	232
A	EVELYN BEACH	24.635/6	142
A	GALAXY VILLAS	22.910	80
A	GOLDEN BEACH	22.391	156
A	HERSONISSOS PALACE	22.777	262
A	KASTRI VILLAGE	22.102	32
A	KING MINOS PALACE	22.781/2	253
A	KOUTOULOUFARI B	22.688	24
A	LYTTOS	22.575/8	601
A	NANA BEACH	22.706	450
A	NENA	22.196	22
A	PALATIA VILLAGE	—	50
A	PEFANA VILLAGE	22.411	129
A	SEMIRAMIS VILLAGE	21.005	172
A	SERITA BEACH	24.542	395
A	SILVA MARIS	22.850/6	401
A	WEST APARTMENTS	22.850/6	26
A	ZORBAS VILLAGE	22.604	290
B	ALEKA-NACIA	—	28

PREFECTURE OF IRAKLEIO - HOTELS

CATEGORY	NAME	TEL. No.	No. of BEDS
B	ALIA	23.146	72
B	ANDROMEDA	—	9
B	ARIANE	22.536	94
B	ASSITES	22.968	20
B	CHRYSSI AMOUDIA	22.971/2	301
B	CRETAN PHILOXENIA	—	
B	NIKOS BEACH	—	103
B	DEDALOS VILLAGE	22.515	98
B	DIANA	—	28
B	DIMITRION	22.220	165
B	ELPIDA HERSONISSOU	—	26
B	GLAROS	22.106	270
B	HARIS	22.346	22
B	HERONISSOS	22.588/9	168
B	HERSONISSOS MARIS	22.354	133
B	IDILIO	—	8
B	IOKASTI	22.607	32
B	KOUTOULOUFARI APART/MS	22.688	42
B	MARAGAKIS	22.405	92
B	MARIA	22.580	66
B	NORA	22.271/5	344
B	OCEANIS	22.671/2	62
B	PHAEDRA HERSONISSOU	—	22
B	PORTO GRECO	—	32
B	SERGIOS	22.583/5	149
B	STELLA VILLAGE	—	142
B	VENUS MELENA	22.892	92
B	VILLES ESPERIDES	22.322/3	98
C	ADAMAKIS	22.447	32
C	ADONIS	22.141	18
C	AGRABELLA	23.110/1	177
C	ALBATROS	22.643/4	182
C	ALEKOS	22.110	14
C	ALOE	22.938	45
C	ALONI	22.562	9
C	ANDRIANI	22.756	24
C	ANGELOS	22.258	23
C	ANNA	22.753	82
C	ANTINOOS	23.142	54
C	ARIADNE	22.312	22
C	ARMAVA	22.544	76
C	ASPA	22.889	12
C	ASPETIS	22.062	24
C	AVERINOS	22.994	58
C	AVRA	22.203	32
C	BIZANTIUM	22.940	50
C	BLUE ISLAND	23.475	66
C	BLUE SKY	22.208	44
C	DIKTINA	22.648/9	72
C	DIMICO	22.697	71
C	DIMITRA	22.225	60
C	ELENI	24.690	23
C	EVA	22.090/2	62
C	FILIPPAKIS	22.165	37
C	FILOXENIA	22.835	30
C	FLISVOS	22.006	118
C	FLORAL	23.004	35
C	GALINI	22.207	56
C	HELEANA	22.830	34
C	HELENA	22.226	24
C	HERCULES	22.527	21
C	ILIOS	22.700	139
C	IRO	22.136	94
C	KATERINA	22.304	34
C	KOSTA MARE	22.297	100
C	KRITIKOS ASTERAS	—	57
C	LENA-MARY	22.907	20
C	MAISTRALI	22.133	27
C	MARIANNA	22.709	94
C	MARIE-CHRISTINE	22.537	80
C	MARIE-GEORGE	22.991	25
C	MARIETA II	22.081	35
C	MARINA	22.041	26
C	MARITA	22.310	31
C	MASTORAKIS	22.965	26
C	MELPO	22.646	77
C	MEMORY	22.497	58
C	MINAS	—	39
C	MIRAMARE	22.796	67
C	NANCY	22.212	49
C	NIKI	22.379/80	57
C	OASSIS	22.932	70
C	PALMERA BEACH	22.481/3	123
C	PARASKEVI	—	31
C	PELA-MARIA	22.195	168
C	PERAKIS	22.968	26
C	PERIGHIALI	—	52
C	PETRA BEACH	23.060	45
C	PISKOPIANO	22.726	41
C	PLAZA	22.760	33

PREFECTURE OF IRAKLEIO - HOTELS

CATEGORY	NAME	TEL. No.	No. of BEDS
C	PSARROS	22.534	33
C	REA	22.357	29
C	REGINA	22.007	22
C	SOFI	22.557	16
C	STELIOS	22.046	35
C	STELLA	22.650	19
C	STELLA PARADISSOS	22.759	24
C	SUN MARINE	24.623	24
C	THALIA	22.590/1	93
C	THEODORA	23.158	29
C	VASSO	22.047	59
C	VELISSARIOS	22.946	41
C	VENUS	23.369	73
C	VILLA IPPOKAMBI	22.316	20
C	VILLA MARGARITA	22.610	43
C	VILLA NELLI	22.962	16
C	VOULA	22.097	26
C	VRITO	22.401	29
C	YANNADAKIS	22.937	16

LINOPERAMATA (2810)

CATEGORY	NAME	TEL. No.	No. of BEDS
A	APOLLONIA BEACH	821.602	590
A	ZEUS BEACH	821.503	717

MALIA (28970)

CATEGORY	NAME	TEL. No.	No. of BEDS
A	IKAROS VILLAGE	31.267/9	326
A	KERNOS BEACH	31.421/5	519
A	KONI	—	26
A	KYKNOS	32.041	98
A	MALIA PARK	31.461/2	378
A	MELISSA	—	18
A	SIRENS BEACH	31.321/5	466
B	ALEXANDER BEACH	32.134	245
B	ANASTASSIA	31.180	44
B	ARIADNE	31.592	59
B	CALYPSO	31.363	78
B	COSTAS	31.485/7	64
B	KOSMIMA MALLION	—	9
B	MALIA BEACH	31.210	354
B	MALIOTAKIS BEACH	—	37
B	MATHEO	—	86
B	NIRIIDES	32.028	28
B	PHAEDRA BEACH	31.560/1	167
B	TRITON	32.210	34

CATEGORY	NAME	TEL. No.	No. of BEDS
C	ALTIS	31.217	33
C	AMVROSSIA	31.378	54
C	ARTEMIS	31.583	45
C	CHRISTIANA BEACH	31.369	46
C	CLEO	31.112	18
C	DIONYSSOS	31.475	27
C	EFI	31.640	35
C	ELKOMI	31.595	55
C	FLORELLA	31.664	56
C	FRIXOS	31.941	64
C	GHIANNIS-MARIA	31.313	18
C	HELEN	31.545	43
C	HERMES	31.788	69
C	ILMA	—	31
C	MALIA HOLIDAYS	31.206	162
C	MALIA MARE	31.809	64
C	MALIA STUDIOS	—	25
C	MARIA-ROUSSE	—	41
C	MINOA	31.456	37
C	MINOIKOS ILIOS	31.106	19
C	MISTRAL	31.934/5	54
C	NEON	31.997/8	48
C	PASSIPHAE	—	37
C	SOFOKLES BEACH	31.348	64
C	SUN BEACH	31.557	57
C	SUNSHINE	31.401	22
C	VERGAS	31.606	38
C	WINDMILL	31.645	39

MATALA (28920)

CATEGORY	NAME	TEL. No.	No. of BEDS
B	ARMONIA	42.735	47
B	VALLEY VILLAGE	42.776	86
C	CALYPSO	42.792	27
C	EVA-MARINA	42.125	40
C	FRANGISKOS	42.380	69
C	KAPETAN NIKOLAS	42.780	33
C	MARINA	42.793	27
C	MATALA BAY	42.100	104
C	ORION	42.129	88
C	PRINGIPISSA EVROPI	42.113	48
C	SUN	42.146	54
C	ZAFIRIA II	42.112	134

NEA ALIKARNASSOS (2810)

CATEGORY	NAME	TEL. No.	No. of BEDS
B	ASTERION	227.913	84

PREFECTURE OF IRAKLEIO - HOTELS

TOWN / AREA CATEGORY	NAME	TEL. No.	No. of BEDS
C	SOFIA	240.002	81

PALEOKASTRO (2810)

C	ROGDIA	821.373	42

PISKOPIANO (28970)

B	KALIMERA	—	44
B	PANORAMA	811.002	156
B	STELVA VILLES	22.890	22
B	VILLES MIKA	22.983	24
C	ANNA-MARIA	22.257	12
C	EDELWEIS	22.631	20
C	KORIFI I	—	26

POROS (2810)

C	GLORIA	288.223/4	95
C	PASSIPHAE	283.135	32
C	POSEIDON	285.859	49
C	PRINCE	287.107	50

SERVILI TILISSOU (2810)

A	AROLITHOS	821.050/3	62

STALIDA (28970)

A	ANTHOUSSA BEACH	31.380/2	309
A	CRETA SOLARIS	31.496	30
A	ILISSIA PEDIA	32.090	32
A	RESIDENCE	31.528	52
B	ALKYONIDES	31.558	54
B	AMAZONES VILLAS	31.488	58
B	BLUE SEA	31.371/3	371
B	CACTUS BEACH	32.494/7	168
B	DIAMOND BEACH	—	34
B	HORIZON BEACH	31.208	106
B	KATRIN	32.137/40	80
B	MARLENA	—	46
B	PALM BEACH	31.666	40
B	PENELOPE	31.370	28
B	SUNNY BEACH	31.587	55
B	ZEPHYROS BEACH	31.566	101
C	CAPTAIN'S VILLA	31.593	37
C	ELVIRA	31.634	35

TOWN / AREA CATEGORY	NAME	TEL. No.	No. of BEDS
C	HELIOTROPE	31.515/7	156
C	KORINA	31.057	32
C	L'AMOUR	31.615	24
C	LATANIA	31.556	13
C	NIKI	31.964	21
C	PANORAMA STALIDOS	31.957/9	20
C	SMARAGDINE BEACH	31.952	16
C	THISVI	31.969	21
C	VILLA ANNA	31.506	26
C	VILLA MARIA	31.450	22
C	VILLA RITSA	31.492	22
C	ZERVAS BEACH	32.719	40

TIMBAKI (28920)

C	AGIOS GEORGIOS	51.678	16

VATHIANOS KAMBOS (2810)

C	MARILIZA	242.905	32

VORI (2810)

B	PATRIKO	—	6

ZAROS (28940)

C	IDI	31.302	111

PREFECTURE OF LASITHI - HOTELS

TOWN / AREA CATEGORY	NAME	TEL. No.	No. of BEDS
AGIA FOTIA (28430)			
B	MARESOL	28.933	47
C	ROMANZA	22.245	12
AGIOS NIKOLAOS (28410)			
L	MINOS BEACH	22.345/9	233
L	MINOS PALACE	23.801/9	276
L	MIRABELLO VILLAGE	28.400/5	251
L	ST. NICOLAS BAY	25.041/3	90
A	ALANTHA	23.527	34
A	ARCHONTIKON	—	20
A	CRETAN VILLAGE	28.576	22
A	HERA VILLAGE	28.971/3	88
A	HERMES	28.253/6	379
A	KALLITHEA	—	60
A	MAR-EGEON	25.513	18
A	MARIANNA	—	28
A	MARNELOS APTS.	25.636	14
A	MIRABELLO	28.400/5	322
A	PORTO DI CANDIA	26.811	387
A	SMARAGDI	—	22
A	TRITON	—	22
B	AFRODITI	28.200	20
B	AGAPI	—	24
B	ALEXANDROS	23.907	16
B	ARIADNI BEACH	22.741/3	142
B	CORAL	28.363/7	323
B	DILINA	28.292	23
B	DIMITRA	23.290	24
B	DOMENICO	22.845	46
B	EL GRECO	28.894	87
B	EVITA	—	10
B	LABYRINTH	23.521	26
B	MANDRAKI	28.880	30
B	MARE	25.144	18
B	MICRO VILLAGE	—	75
B	MIRAMARE	22.962	100
B	OLGA	23.932	54
B	ORMOS	24.094	86
B	RENAISSANCE	22.125	44
B	RHEA	28.321/3	220
B	SAND APARTMENTS	28.452	56
B	SANTA MARINA	26.261/5	241
B	SOFIA	24.690	28

TOWN / AREA CATEGORY	NAME	TEL. No.	No. of BEDS
B	SUNLIGHT	26.622	31
C	ACRATOS	22.721/5	59
C	ALCESTIS	22.454	45
C	ALFA	23.701	74
C	ALMYROS BEACH	22.865/6	87
C	AMALTHIA	28.914/5	38
C	ANTZELA	22.008	20
C	APOLLON	23.023/5	114
C	ARTEMIS BEACH	22.065	33
C	ASTORIA	25.148	50
C	ATHINA	28.225	33
C	BELLA VISTA	—	20
C	CARAVEL	28.937	28
C	CASTLE	24.918	10
C	CHRISTINA SIDERIS	—	55
C	CRETA STAR	23.845	39
C	CRI-CRI	23.720	30
C	CRONOS	28.761/2	68
C	CRYSTAL	24.407	56
C	DIANA	22.694	31
C	DIAS	28.263/4	25
C	DOXA	24.214	38
C	DU LAX	22.711/2	60
C	ELECTRA	25.211	44
C	ELENA	28.189	77
C	EVA	22.587	12
C	GEFYRA	28.566	30
C	GERANI	—	30
C	HAVANIA	28.758	50
C	HELEN-NIK	—	25
C	IDRIA	—	20
C	IKAROS	28.901/3	35
C	ILIOS	—	54
C	IRIS	22.407	41
C	KAMARA	23.717	51
C	KNOSSOS	24.871	24
C	KOUROS	23.264	47
C	LATO	24.581/2	48
C	LEVENTIS	22.423	17
C	LIDA	22.130	40
C	LITO	23.067	71
C	LOTZIA	—	34
C	MAGDA	23.925	47
C	MARIELLA	24.698	25
C	MARIGO	28.439	24

PREFECTURE OF LASITHI - HOTELS

CATEGORY	TOWN / AREA NAME	TEL. No.	No. of BEDS
C	MAVROFOROS	23.714	21
C	MELAS APARTMENTS	28.734	31
C	MINOAN APARTMENTS	—	12
C	MOUSSES	61.446	36
C	MYRSINI	28.590	60
C	NIKI	22.095	20
C	NIKOS	24.464	71
C	ODYSSEAS	23.934	35
C	PANGALOS	22.936	43
C	PANORAMA	28.890	56
C	PARADISE VILLA	28.031	15
C	POSSIDONAS	24.086	54
C	SGOUROS	28.931	48
C	SUNRISE	—	16
C	TRANTAS	—	12
C	VICTORIA	22.731	28
C	VLASSIS	—	90
C	ZINA	22.210	33

AMOUDARA (28410)

CATEGORY	NAME	TEL. No.	No. of BEDS
B	ALKYON	24.495/7	58
B	VIRGINIA	22.782	38
C	DIMITRIS BEACH	—	21
C	FILIPPOS	22.761	30
C	MARIANTHI	28.873	30
C	POLYDOROS	22.623	11
C	STELLA	—	29

ELOUNDA (28410)

CATEGORY	NAME	TEL. No.	No. of BEDS
L	ASTIR PALACE ELOUNDA BAY	41.580/4	551
L	ELOUNDA BEACH	41.812	578
L	ELOUNDA MARE	41.102/3	200
A	ELOUDA ILION	41.703	74
A	ELOUNDA GULF VILLAS	41.279	52
A	ELOUNDA MARMIN	41.513	295
A	ELOUNDA RESIDENCE	41.823	74
A	ELOUNDA ROCK	41.802	316
A	SPINALONGA VILLAGE	41.494/6	34
B	ARMOS	41.158/9	90
B	DRIROS BEACH	41.283	36
B	ELOUNDA BLUE BAY	41.924	180
B	ELOUNDA ISLAND VILLAS	—	23
B	ELOUNDA PALM	41.825	98

CATEGORY	TOWN / AREA NAME	TEL. No.	No. of BEDS
B	ESPEROS	41.613	36
C	AKTI OLOUS	41.720/1	95
C	ANGELIKI	41.466	29
C	ARISTEA	41.300/5	62
C	CALYPSO	41.367	30
C	KATERINA	41.484	17
C	KORFOS BEACH	41.591	29
C	KRINI	41.602	61
C	ORIZON	41.895	29
C	SELENA VILLAGE	41.525	98
C	SOPHIA	41.482	26

FERMA (28420)

CATEGORY	NAME	TEL. No.	No. of BEDS
A	THALASSA	61.352/6	289
B	CORIVA VILLAGE	61.263	69
B	KAKKOS BAY	—	79
B	PORTO BELISSARIO	61.358/9	63
C	OASSIS	23.536	26

IERAPETRA (28420)

CATEGORY	NAME	TEL. No.	No. of BEDS
A	CASTRO CALES	23.858	13
A	CRETAN HOUSES	61.409	78
A	DI MARE	23.502	28
A	ELYROS VILLAGE	61.500	300
A	KOUTSOUNARI TRADITIONAL COTTA	61.291	39
A	LYKTOS BEACH RESORT HOTEL	61.280	421
A	PETRA MARE	23.341/9	405
B	BLUE SKY	28.264	45
B	KOTHRIS	24.180	36
B	MINOAN PRINCE	24.192	105
B	OSTRIA BEACH	25.711/4	103
B	SUNRISE	—	28
C	ACHLIA	61.306/7	51
C	ASTRON	25.114	142
C	ATLANTIS	—	134
C	CAMIROS	28.704	75
C	COSMO	25.900	50
C	EL GRECO	28.471	62
C	ERSI	23.208/9	25
C	GALAXY	26.541/3	97
C	KOUTSOUNARI HORIO NAKOU	61.291	13

PREFECTURE OF LASITHI - HOTELS

TOWN / AREA			
CATEGORY	NAME	TEL. No.	No. of BEDS
C	KYRVA	22.594	56
C	LYGIA	28.881/2	29
C	VARMY	23.059/60	27
C	ZAKROS	24.101/3	88

KALO HORIO (28410)

L	ISTRON BAY	61.303	215
A	KLIO	—	14
B	MISTRAL	61.134	128
C	ELPIDA	61.403	168
C	GOLDEN BAY	61.202	94

MIRTOS (28420)

C	ESPERIDES	—	54
C	MERTIZA	51.208	37
C	MYRTOS	51.215	32
C	PETROVILLA	51.483	12

MOHLOS (28430)

B	ALDIANA CLUB	94.211/3	262

PAHIA AMOS (28420)

C	GOLDEN BEACH	93.278	22

PALEKASTRO (28430)

C	HELLAS	61.240	24

PALEOKASTRO (28430)

C	MARINA VILLAGE	61.284/5	62

SISSI (28410)

A	HELLENIC PALACE	71.502	179
A	MARTIMO	71.257	132
A	PORTO SISSI	71.385	30
A	SISSI BAY	71.284	26
A	SISSI MARE	71.120	36
B	AMADEUS	—	34
B	CASTELLO VILLAGE I	71.367	88
B	KOUTRAKIS APTS	—	46

TOWN / AREA			
CATEGORY	NAME	TEL. No.	No. of BEDS
C	ANTZELA	71.121	29
C	CASTELLO VILLAGE II	71.367	89
C	CHRISTI-MARIE	71.360	25
C	CHRISTINA-EVINA	—	68
C	ESPERIDES	—	54
C	SISSI BAY I	71.284	22
C	SISSI BAY III	71.284	130
C	SISSI ROCK	71.125	84
C	VILLES KANETOU	—	16
C	ZYGOS	71.279	24

SITIA (28430)

A	PAN MAR	51.775	14
A	SITIA BEACH	28.821/7	310
A	SUNWING I	51.621/4	368
A	WHITE RIVER COTTAGES	51.120	21
B	SUNWING II	51.621	191
B	VILLEA VILLAGE	51.697	116
C	ALICE	28.450	69
C	BELLE VUE	—	22
C	CASTELLO	23.763	31
C	CRYSTAL	22.284	75
C	DENIS	28.356	25
C	EL GRECO	23.133	28
C	ELYSEE	23.427	45
C	GOLDEN SUN	51.679	60
C	HELENA	22.681	42
C	ITANOS	22.146	138
C	MARIANA	22.088	47
C	OKEANIDES	—	15
C	PHOENIX	28.100	15
C	SOUTH COAST	51.446	113
C	SUN RISE	—	16
C	SUNWING III	51.002	192
C	VAI	22.288	84

TZERMIADO (28440)

C	KOURITES	22.194	

ZAKROS (28430)

C	ZAKROS	93.379	30